Friedrich Katz

Wiener Vorlesungen: Forschungen

Herausgegeben für die Kulturabteilung der Stadt Wien
von Hubert Christian Ehalt

Band 6

Die in diesem Band versammelten Essays sind dem Historiker und Lateinamerikanisten Friedrich Katz (1927-2010) gewidmet. Sie fußen auf einem Symposium, das im Herbst 2011 zu seinen Ehren in Wien abgehalten wurde, und vereinen unterschiedliche Perspektiven auf sein Leben und Werk. Friedrich Katz war einer der großen Sozialhistoriker zur lateinamerikanischen Geschichte des 20. Jahrhunderts. Seine Arbeiten zur Mexikanischen Revolution zählen zu den grundlegenden Werken über dieses Thema. Er verstand es, in quellenkritischer Tiefe die Besonderheiten Mexikos in die Weltgeschichte einzuschreiben. Andererseits verschlug eben diese Weltgeschichte ihn selbst als Kind von Wien über Berlin, Paris und New York nach Mexiko, nach 1945 wieder nach Wien und Ostberlin und schließlich nach Chicago.

The essays collected in this volume are dedicated to the historian and Latin Americanist Friedrich Katz (1927-2010). They are based on a symposium held in his honour in Vienna in the autumn of 2011 and bring together varying perspectives of his life and work. As one of the great social historians of our time, Friedrich Katz had an encyclopaedic knowledge of the sources relevant to Latin America's twentieth century history. His studies of the Mexican Revolution rank foremost among contributions to the field. More than anyone before he succeeded in relating the specifics of Mexico's history to the broader processes of global history. That same global history impacted repeatedly on Katz' own life: he was forced to leave Vienna as a child and moved with his family to Mexico, via Berlin, Paris and New York; he returned to Vienna after 1945 only to leave again for East Berlin before finally settling in Chicago.

Martina Kaller, Philosophin und Historikerin, ist Professorin für Geschichte der Neuzeit an der Universität Wien.
David Mayer und Berthold Molden sind Historiker an der Universität Wien.

Martina Kaller, philosopher and historian, is professor of Modern History at the University of Vienna.
David Mayer and Berthold Molden are historians at the University of Vienna.

PETER LANG
Frankfurt am Main · Berlin · Bern · Bruxelles · New York · Oxford · Wien

Martina Kaller
David Mayer
Berthold Molden
(Hrsg.)

Friedrich Katz

Essays zu Leben und Wirken eines transnationalen Historikers

Essays on the Life and Work of a Transnational Historian

PETER LANG
Internationaler Verlag der Wissenschaften

Bibliografische Information der Deutschen Nationalbibliothek
Die Deutsche Nationalbibliothek verzeichnet diese Publikation in der Deutschen Nationalbibliografie; detaillierte bibliografische Daten sind im Internet über http://dnb.d-nb.de abrufbar.

Umschlaggestaltung:
Hubert Christian Ehalt

ISSN 1437-9015
ISBN 978-3-631-63776-0

Internationaler Verlag der Wissenschaften
Frankfurt am Main 2012

www.peterlang.de

Die Wiener Vorlesungen im Rathaus

Die Wiener Vorlesungen laden seit Anfang 1987 wichtige Persönlichkeiten des intellektuellen Lebens dazu ein, in den Festsälen des Rathauses ihre Analysen und Befunde zu den großen aktuellen Problemen der Welt vorzulegen. Seither sind diese Vorträge das Dialogforum der Stadt Wien, eine Stadtuniversität, öffentlich, frei zugänglich und immer am Puls der Zeit.

Bei 1.200 Veranstaltungen waren bisher weit mehr als 5.000 Referentinnen und Referenten und über 600.000 Zuhörerinnen und Zuhörer. Zur Diskussion stehen immer die zentralen Fragen, denen die Welt gegenübersteht. Die ReferentInnen, die von den Wiener Vorlesungen um Analyse, Befund und Expertise gebeten werden, sind die Besten ihres Faches.

Die Zielsetzung der Wiener Vorlesungen ist die aktuelle Weiterführung des Projektes der Aufklärung. Es geht nicht nur um Wissen als Information, sondern Wissen als Auseinandersetzung und Kritik, die dazu beitragen, „Bildung" als individuelle und kollektive Qualität des Wissens und der Erkenntnis weiterzuentwickeln. „Sapere aude", das Wagnis des Wissens als verantwortungsbewusste und mutige Haltung und Handlung gegen eingefahrene und ritualisierte Konventionen ist wie im 18. Jahrhundert bei den Vordenkern der Aufklärung auch das zentrale Postulat der Wiener Vorlesungen. Philosophie und Methode des Projektes lassen sich in acht Punkten zusammenfassen. Aufklärung statt Vernebelung, Differenzierung statt Vereinfachung, Analyse statt Infotainment, Tiefenschärfe statt Oberflächenpolitur, Empathie statt Egomanie, Utopien statt Fortschreibung, Widerspruch statt Anpassung, Auseinandersetzung statt Belehrung. Die gegenwärtige Welt braucht Kritik und Perspektive im Sinne dieses Programms. Wirtschaft, Gesellschaft, Politik und Kultur müssen – das zeigen die gegenwärtigen Probleme im Zusammenhang mit den aktuellen Wirtschafts- und Bankenkrisen in aller Deutlichkeit – neu gedacht werden. Nie wurde so deutlich wie in den letzten Jahren, dass routinemäßige Fortschreibung nicht mehr möglich ist.

Die Methode, mit der die Wiener Vorlesungen Aufklärung betreiben, ist eine Schärfung des Blicks für die Komplexität, Differenziertheit und – häufig auch – Widersprüchlichkeit dessen, was als gesellschaftliche, kulturelle und politische Wirklichkeit erlebt wird. Der analytisch-interpretative Zugang der Wiener Vorlesungen dämpft die Emotionen und legt Fundamente für eine Bewältigung der Probleme mit zivilen und demokratischen Mitteln. Das Publikum trägt durch seine Teilnahme an den Wiener Vorlesungen zur Verbreitung jenes „Virus" bei, das für ein gutes politisches Klima verantwortlich ist.

Unter den bisherigen Referentinnen und Referenten befanden sich u.a. Marie Albu-Jahoda, Kofi Annan, Aleida Assmann, Jan Assmann, Jean Baudrillard, Ulrich Beck, Hans Belting, Bruno Bettelheim, Leon Botstein, Pierre Bourdieu, Christina von Braun, Elisabeth Bronfen, Ernesto Cardenal, Luc Ciompi, Carl Djerassi, Marion Dönhoff, Barbara Duden, Irenäus Eibl-Eibesfeldt, Manfred Eigen, Mario Erdheim, Amitai Etzioni, Valie Export, Vilem Flusser, Heinz von Foerster, Viktor Frankl, Peter Gay, Ute Gerhard, Maurice Godelier, Ernst Gombrich, Michail Gorbatschow, Marianne Gronemeyer, Jürgen Habermas, Nikolaus Harnoncourt, Karin Hausen, Jeanne Hersch, Eric J. Hobsbawm, Werner Hofmann, Ivan Illich, Eric Kandel, Verena Kast, Friedrich Katz, Otto F. Kernberg, Rudolf Kirchschläger, Václav Klaus, Ruth Klüger, Teddy Kollek, Kardinal Franz König, György Konrad, Bischof Erwin Kräutler, Bruno Kreisky, Peter Kubelka, Hermann Lübbe, Niklas Luhmann, Viktor Matejka, Dennis L. Meadows, Adam Michnik, Hans Mommsen, Josef Penninger, Roger Penrose, Max F. Perutz, Hugo Portisch, Uta Ranke-Heinemann, Eva Reich, Marcel Reich-Ranicki, Horst-Eberhard Richter, Jeremy Rifkin, Erwin Ringel, Carl E. Schorske, Richard Sennett, Edward Shorter, Dorothee Sölle, Aminata Traoré, Marcel Tshiamalenga Ntumba, Desmond Tutu, Paul Watzlawick, Georg Weidenfeld, Erika Weinzierl, Ruth Wodak, Anton Zeilinger, Hans Zeisel, Jean Ziegler.

Im Sinne des skizzierten Konzeptes war der renommierte Historiker Friedrich Katz im Frühjahr 2004 Vortragender bei den Wiener Vorlesungen zum Thema „Österreich – Mexiko 1938: die stillen Helden der mexikanischen Diplomatie". Im Rahmen dieser Wiener Vorlesung würdigte auch die Universität ihren berühmten Absolventen durch die Überreichung des Goldenen Doktordiploms.

Herr Prof. Katz gehörte zu jenen wenigen Lateinamerika-Forschern, die für die Entwicklung und Akzentuierung des europäischen Forschungsinteresses an Lateinamerika besonders wichtig gewesen sind. Friedl Katz war fraglos ein wichtiger „Entwicklungshelfer" der Lateinamerikaforschung in Österreich.

Nach seinem Tod haben die Wiener Vorlesungen am 20.10.2011 gemeinsam mit der Botschaft von Mexiko und der Universität Wien der Persönlichkeit und dem Werk von Friedrich Katz ein Symposion gewidmet. Als Koordinator der Wiener Vorlesungen bin ich sehr froh darüber, dass die spannenden Beiträge des Symposions nun im vorliegenden Band der Reihe „Wiener Vorlesungen.

Forschungen“ für eine größere Öffentlichkeit erschlossen werden. Der Band ruft die eindrucksvolle Persönlichkeit von Friedl Katz in Erinnerung, stärkt die Verbindung zwischen österreichischer und lateinamerikanischer Forschung und ist damit auch ein Impuls für ein Forschungsfeld, das eine Stärkung sehr gut vertragen kann.

Hubert Christian Ehalt

The Wiener Vorlesungen at the Rathaus

The Wiener Vorlesungen (Vienna Public Lectures) have served since early 1987 as a platform where outstanding exponents of intellectual life can put forward their analyses and views on the world's most topical problems in the festive ambience of Vienna's Town Hall. These lectures have long been the City of Vienna's public discussion forum, a civic university, freely accessible and with an empathic appreciation of the pulse of the times.

To date, 1,200 lectures featuring more than 5,000 lecturers have attracted a total audience of more than 600,000. At the heart of each debate one always finds the key issues confronting the world at the time, and the lecturers invited by the Wiener Vorlesungen to offer their analyses, findings and expert opinions invariably rank at the very top of their respective fields.

The aim of the Wiener Vorlesungen is to do their bit towards keeping the flame first lit by the Enlightenment burning. The lectures focus on knowledge – not on knowledge reduced to mere information but on knowledge of the kind that results from the fruitful exchange between different points of view and from constructive criticism, knowledge that is capable of fostering that independence of thought which is essential for individual and collective wellbeing. „Sapere aude", the motto of the 18th-century pioneers of the Enlightenment, who recommended the courageous use of reason as the primary source of responsible action against stale and ritualized conventions, is the key postulate of the Wiener Vorlesungen. The project's philosophy and method can be summarized in eight points: substitute enlightenment for obfuscation, intellectual challenge for dumbing down, analysis for infotainment, substance for affectation, empathy for self-obsession, progress for stagnation, argument for acquiescence, and the robust exchange of views for indoctrination. The contemporary world needs the criticism and sense of perspective outlined in this programme. As is evident from the conflicts that surface in the context of the current economic and banking crisis, our traditional positions with respect to our economy, society, politics and culture all need a drastic overhaul. It has never been as clear as over the last few years that it is quite simply no longer an option to keep wallowing in an embrace of the status quo.

The method used by the Wiener Vorlesungen to advance this enlightenment project is to foster a clearer perception of the complexity of the social, cultural and political reality as experienced by all of us living today, its daunting challenges and its frequent non-sequiturs. The analytical and interpretative approach of the Wiener Vorlesungen has a sobering effect on the emotions and creates the space we need for problem solving by civil and democratic means. Their participation in the Wiener Vorlesungen allows the audience to contribute their share to the free interchange of ideas that is indispensable for a stable political climate.

Past lecturers have included Marie Albu-Jahoda, Kofi Annan, Aleida Assmann, Jan Assmann, Jean Baudrillard, Ulrich Beck, Hans Belting, Bruno Bettelheim, Leon Botstein, Pierre Bourdieu, Christina von Braun, Elisabeth Bronfen, Ernesto Cardenal, Luc Ciompi, Carl Djerassi, Marion Dönhoff, Barbara Duden, Irenäus Eibl-Eibesfeldt, Manfred Eigen, Mario Erdheim, Amitai Etzioni, Valie Export, Vilem Flusser, Heinz von Foerster, Viktor Frankl, Peter Gay, Ute Gerhard, Maurice Godelier, Ernst Gombrich, Michail Gorbatschow, Marianne Gronemeyer, Jürgen Habermas, Nikolaus Harnoncourt, Karin Hausen, Jeanne Hersch, Eric J. Hobsbawm, Werner Hofmann, Ivan Illich, Eric Kandel, Verena Kast, Friedrich Katz, Otto F. Kernberg, Rudolf Kirchschläger, Václav Klaus, Ruth Klüger, Teddy Kollek, Kardinal Franz König, György Konrad, Bishop Erwin Kräutler, Bruno Kreisky, Peter Kubelka, Hermann Lübbe, Niklas Luhmann, Viktor Matejka, Dennis L. Meadows, Adam Michnik, Hans Mommsen, Josef Penninger, Roger Penrose, Max F. Perutz, Hugo Portisch, Uta Ranke-Heinemann, Eva Reich, Marcel Reich-Ranicki, Horst-Eberhard Richter, Jeremy Rifkin, Erwin Ringel, Carl E. Schorske, Richard Sennett, Edward Shorter, Dorothee Sölle, Aminata Traoré, Marcel Tshiamalenga Ntumba, Bishop Desmond Tutu, Paul Watzlawick, Georg Weidenfeld, Erika Weinzierl, Ruth Wodak, Anton Zeilinger, Hans Zeisel, and Jean Ziegler.

It is a matter of pride for us and in keeping with the concept of the Wiener Vorlesungen as outlined above that the renowned historian Friedrich Katz gave a lecture here in spring 2004 on the topic „Österreich – Mexiko 1938: die stillen Helden der mexikanischen Diplomatie“ [Austria – Mexico 1938: the quiet heroes of Mexican diplomacy]. It was on the occasion of this Vienna Public Lecture that the University paid tribute to its famous alumnus by awarding him his Golden Doctoral Diploma.

Professor Katz belongs to that select group of Americanists who have left their stamp on the development and diversification of the European research interest in Latin America. Friedl Katz was undoubtedly an important "aid worker" who has been a great stimulus for Americanist Studies in Austria.

After his death in 2010 the Embassy of Mexico, the University of Vienna and the Wiener Vorlesungen jointly organized a symposium on October 20, 2011 in honour of Friedrich Katz and his work. In my capacity as the coordinator of the Wiener Vorlesungen I welcome the publication of the exciting papers presented at the symposium in this volume of the series „Wiener Vorlesungen. Forschungen“. The intention behind this volume is to pay homage to a great scholar, to strengthen the ties between the scholarly communities in Austria and in Mexico and to provide encouragement to a field of research in Austria that can use all the encouragement it can get.

Hubert Christian Ehalt

Inhaltsverzeichnis

Vorwort der HerausgeberInnen 15

Editors' Preface 17

Friedrich Katz: Vielseitiger Historiker und Wahlmexikaner 19
Javier Garciadiego

Friedrich Katz: Versatile historian and Mexican by adoption 27
Javier Garciadiego

Friedrich Katz an der Universität Wien. Von der Exzellenz ins Nichts 35
Martina Kaller

Friedrich Katz at the University of Vienna. From Excellence to Non-Existence 45
Martina Kaller

Biographische Fragmente. Friedrich Katz – Erinnerungen ans mexikanische Exil 55
Christian Kloyber

Friedrich Katz – Memories of the Mexican Exile 65
Christian Kloyber

Der Weltenläufer: Friedrich Katz und die historiographischen Debatten seiner Zeit 73
David Mayer

Well-Versed in Worlds: Friedrich Katz and the historiographical debates of his time 85
David Mayer

Die Selbstermächtigung der Maus. Friedrich Katz und das Überleben 97
Berthold Molden

The Self-Empowerment of the Mouse. The life and survival of Friedrich Katz 107
Berthold Molden

Autorin und Autoren 117

Vorwort der HerausgeberInnen

Dieses Buch ist das Ergebnis eines Nachmittages im Oktober 2011, der im Rahmen der *Wiener Vorlesungen* dem Leben und Werk von Friedrich Katz gewidmet war. Im Senatssitzungssaal des Alten Rathauses in Wiens Innerer Stadt referierten und diskutierten Javier Garciadiego, Direktor des Colegio de México, und die Wiener Historiker David Mayer und Berthold Molden mit Martina Kaller und Zeitzeugen, darunter Friedrich Katz' Tochter Jacqueline Ross. Persönliche Erinnerungen an den einflussreichen Mexikanisten hatten ebenso Raum wie die wissenschaftshistorische Einschätzung seines Werks. So gedachten ein Jahr nach dem Tod von Katz die Stadt Wien, die mexikanische Botschaft in Österreich und die Universität Wien eines jener „großen Söhne", der hier mindestens soviel Ablehnung wie Anerkennung erfuhr und doch die Zuneigung für seine Geburtsstadt bis zuletzt bewahrte.

In gewisser Weise – bereichert um eine mexikanische Perspektive – ist dieses Buch ein Blick von Wiener HistorikerInnen auf einen großen Kollegen, der aus dieser Stadt hervorgegangen und nicht wieder dahin zurückgekehrt ist. Es ist in weiten Teilen die Geschichte der Kontingenzen und Wechselfälle einer intellektuellen Biographie in den Konflikten des 20. Jahrhunderts, eine Geschichte von Möglichkeiten und Entscheidungen, von Gelungenem und von Versäumtem. Friedrich Katz ist Markstein und Messlatte unserer Zunft als einer der großen Sozialhistoriker zur mexikanischen Geschichte des 20. Jahrhunderts, der es verstand, in quellenkritischer Tiefe die Besonderheiten dieses Landes in die Weltgeschichte einzuschreiben. Andererseits verschlug eben diese Weltgeschichte ihn selbst als Kind von Wien über Berlin, Paris und New York nach Mexiko, nach 1945 wieder nach Wien und Ost-Berlin und schließlich nach Chicago. In Wien über Friedrich Katz zu sprechen, heißt sich auf die Geschichte dieser Stadt, ihrer Universität, ihrer politischen und intellektuellen Milieus und ihres Platzes in der Globalgeschichte des 20. Jahrhunderts einzulassen.

Der Gastgeber der *Wiener Vorlesungen*, Christian Ehalt, ist selbst Historiker und mit Friedrich Katz auch dadurch verbunden, dass er namens der Stadt Wien im März 2004 anlässlich der Verleihung des Goldenen Doktordiploms für das 50jährige Jubiläum von Katz' Promotion an der Universität Wien eine Feier im Rathaus ausrichtete. Dies blieb zu Lebzeiten Katz' eine der wenigen Anerkennungen in einer Reihe von Unterlassungen seitens der Universität Wien und des offiziellen Österreich. Mit dem Symposium „Hommage an Friedrich Katz" am

20. Oktober 2011 und dem vorliegenden Band soll dies zumindest posthum ausgeglichen werden.

Javier Garciadiego, Schüler, enger Freund von Katz und selbst zentraler Akteur der mexikanischen Geschichtswissenschaft, erklärt die Bedeutung von Katz für das Geschichtsdenken in dessen geliebtem Exilland, dem er sein gesamtes Lebenswerk widmete. Christian Kloyber, mit der Familie Katz ebenso persönlich wie über emigrationshistorische Studien verbunden, beleuchtet ihre mexikanische Erfahrung aus der Perspektive seines eigenen Werdegangs.

Martina Kaller studierte die Akten im Archiv der Universität Wien und belegt, wie die politischen Altlasten Österreichs eine akademische Karriere von Friedrich Katz in seiner Heimatstadt vereitelten. David Mayer und Berthold Molden vertreten in diesem Band die lateinamerikanistische Geschichtswissenschaft an der Universität Wien und richten ihre Aufmerksamkeit auf unterschiedliche Aspekte des „Weltenlaufs" (David Mayer) von Friedrich Katz und dessen Tangenten zu Wien: Katz und die geschichtswissenschaftlichen Debatten seiner Zeit zwischen Wien, Berlin, Mexiko und Chicago; und Katz, der Überlebende, Remigrant und als jüdischer Kommunist aus dem Nachkriegswien abermals „Vertriebene".

Das Symposium im Herbst 2011 wurde in Kooperation zwischen der Stadt Wien, der Universität Wien und der mexikanischen Botschaft in Österreich ermöglicht. Diesen Institutionen sei ebenso gedankt wie Christian Ehalt, der die Herausgabe dieses Bandes tatkräftig unterstützte. Dank gilt auch dem Übersetzer Otmar Binder, der zusammen mit David Sinclair-Jones die englische Fassung der Beiträge besorgte.

Biographie und Werk von Friedrich Katz rufen in Erinnerung, welche Verluste Wien aufgrund von Vertreibung und Vernichtung durch den Nationalsozialismus zu gewärtigen hatte. Sie zeigen auch, wie eng die geistige und politische Atmosphäre im Nachkriegsösterreich war und wie wenig diese Vertriebenen willkommen geheißen wurden. Katz verkörperte inhaltlich jenen Anti-Provinzialismus, der heute in den historischen Wissenschaften allenthalben gefordert wird. Das Gedenken an ihn mag als Bekenntnis zu weltoffener und perspektivenpluraler Forschung dienen. Die Einrichtung eines Friedrich Katz-Chair für historische Lateinamerikaforschung an der Universität Wien wäre der angemessene institutionelle Ausdruck eines solchen Bekenntnisses.

Martina Kaller David Mayer Berthold Molden

Editors' Preface

This book is the fruit of an afternoon devoted to Friedrich Katz' life and work in the *Wiener Vorlesungen* series of lectures in October 2011. In the Senate Assembly Hall of Vienna's Old Town Hall in the city centre the director of the Colegio de México, Javier Garciadiego, and the Viennese historians David Mayer and Berthold Molden each presented a paper and engaged in discussion with Martina Kaller and contemporary witnesses, who included Friedrich Katz' daughter Jacqueline Ross. There was room for personal memories of the late expert in Mexican Studies and for a rough thumb sketch of the history of the discipline to indicate the rank Katz holds within it. Representatives of the City of Vienna, Mexico's Embassy in Vienna and the University of Vienna together remembered one of the city's "great sons", who had met at least with as much rejection here as acceptance; this however did not prevent him from retaining a place in his heart of hearts for the city of his birth.

This book represents a take by Viennese historians, which benefits from an additional Mexican perspective, on a great colleague who came from this city and chose not to return to it. It attempts to convey the contingencies and vicissitudes of an outstanding intellectual's life that bears testimony to the key conflicts of the twentieth century and was shaped in turn by the opportunities and decisions and the many successes and failures resulting from these conflicts. One of the great social historians of our time, Friedrich Katz had an encyclopaedic knowledge of the sources relevant to Mexico's twentieth century history. Wearing it lightly, he used it to maximum effect, with the result that the specifics of Mexico's history are now considered to be part of global history. That same global history impacted repeatedly on Katz' own life. He was forced to leave Vienna as a child and ultimately moved with his family to Mexico, via Berlin, Paris and New York; he returned to Vienna after 1945 only to leave again for East Berlin before finally settling in Chicago. Talking about Friedrich Katz in Vienna involves addressing also the history of this city, of its university, its political and intellectual milieus and of its place in twentieth century global history.

Christian Ehalt, himself a historian by profession and in charge of the *Wiener Vorlesungen*, is explicitly linked to Friedrich Katz by hosting on behalf of the City of Vienna an event at the Town Hall in March 2004 to celebrate the award of the Golden Doctoral Diploma to Katz on the 50th anniversary of his graduation from the University of Vienna. This was one of the few acknowledgements granted to Katz during his lifetime by the University and official Austria. The symposium "Hommage an Friedrich Katz" on October 20, 2011 and the present volume are attempts to set this relationship at least posthumously on a more even keel.

Javier Garciadiego, one of Katz' former students and a close friend, is a key exponent of Mexican historiography; in this volume he gauges the impact Katz had on historical thinking in the country that offered him refuge and is the dedicatee of his life's work. Christian Kloyber, author of studies in the history of emigration and befriended by Katz and his family, casts a revealing light on their Mexican experience from a more personal point of view.

Martina Kaller documents on the basis of files in the archives of the University of Vienna how Austria's neglected post-war deposits of politically toxic waste made it impossible for Katz to launch himself on an academic career in the city of his birth. David Mayer and Berthold Molden, both exponents of Latin-American historiography at the University of Vienna, focus on different aspects of Katz as a roving historian and his tangential contacts with Vienna: Katz and the historiographical debates of his time in Vienna, Berlin, Mexico and Chicago; and Katz the survivor and returning emigrant who was expelled again from post-war Vienna as a Jewish communist.

The symposium in the autumn of 2011 was a collaborative venture by the City of Vienna, Vienna University and the Mexican Embassy in Austria for which we would like to thank these institutions. We also want to acknowledge our gratitude to Christian Ehalt, who has contributed substantially to making this publication possible. Our thanks also go to Otmar Binder and David Sinclair-Jones, who were in charge of the translation work.

Friedrich Katz' life and work may serve as vivid reminders of the losses Vienna incurred owing to the persecution and extermination policies of the Nazis. By the same token we are reminded of the intellectual and political narrowness of post-war Austria and of its unwillingness to welcome back the survivors of these policies. In terms of the content of his research, Katz embodied that anti-provincialism that is now being proclaimed everywhere as an indispensable prerequisite in the historical sciences. Cultivating the memory of Katz certainly amounts to an endorsement of a cosmopolitan and multiperspectival type of research. The establishment of a Friedrich Katz Chair for Research on the History of Latin America would be the institutionally adequate counterpart of such an endorsement.

Martina Kaller David Mayer Berthold Molden

Friedrich Katz: Vielseitiger Historiker und Wahlmexikaner

Javier Garciadiego

Am 16. Oktober 2010 starb Friedrich Katz. Bis heute zählt er zu den weltweit bekanntesten Historikern. Er war Autor zweier echter Klassiker der Geschichtsschreibung der Mexikanischen Revolution: *The Secret War in Mexico*[1] und *The Life and Times of Pancho Villa*.[2] Als jüngster von vielen Belegen für die hohe Anerkennung seiner akademischen Arbeit wurde Katz zum Ehrenpräsidenten des XIII. Treffens der Historiker Mexikos, der USA und Kanadas in der Stadt Querétaro im Oktober 2010 ernannt. Er nahm diese Ehre voll Demut an, konnte aber wegen seines kritischen Gesundheitszustands nicht mehr persönlich an der Konferenz teilnehmen. Katz starb zehn Tage, bevor die Tagung begann. Das Leben von Friedrich Katz war so kosmopolitisch wie seine diplomatiegeschichtliche Sicht auf die Mexikanische Revolution. Seine Kindheit und frühe Jugend waren turbulent wie das Leben von Pancho Villa, den er sehr bewunderte, was auch in seiner Biographie des Revolutionärs zum Ausdruck kommt.

Friedrich Katz stammte aus Wien. Sein Vater, Leo Katz, kämpfte als Journalist gegen Hitler und den Nationalsozialismus. Als Hitler 1933 in Deutschland an die Macht kam, musste die Familie nach Frankreich flüchten, von wo sie zu Beginn des Zweiten Weltkriegs ebenfalls ausgewiesen wurde. Die Eltern und ihr einziger Sohn gingen nach New York. Da sie nur ein Touristenvisum für ein Jahr hatten und die Rückkehr nach Europa für sie lebensgefährlich gewesen wäre, mussten sie neuerlich Zuflucht suchen. 1940 erreichten sie Mexiko, wo auf Initiative von Präsident Lázaro Cárdenas zahlreichen politischen Exilanten aus Zentraleuropa und Spanien Asyl gewährt wurde. Friedrich Katz war damals 13 Jahre alt. Sein bisheriges Leben war gezeichnet von Verfolgung und Ablehnung, die er nicht verstehen konnte. Im Verlauf dieser zwar kurzen, aber doch intensiven Erfahrungen hatte er neben der deutschen Muttersprache bereits zwei weitere Sprachen erlernen müssen. In der französisch-mexikanischen Schule in Mexiko kam nun mit Spanisch eine weitere hinzu.

---

[1] Katz, Friedrich: *The Secret War in Mexico. Europe, the United States and the Mexican revolution*, University of Chicago Press, Chicago u.a. 1981. Katz, Friedrich: *La Guerra Secreta en México*, 2 Bde., ERA, México, D.F. 1982.

[2] Katz, Friedrich: *The Life and Times of Pancho Villa*, Stanford University Press, Stanford 1998. Katz, Friedrich: *Pancho Villa*, 2 Bde., ERA, México, D.F. 1998.

Friedl – so nannten ihn die deutschsprachigen Freunde – erhielt, mehr zu Hause als in der Schule, seine ersten Grundkenntnisse der mexikanischen Geschichte vermittelt: ein Thema, das ihm von Beginn an nahe ging. 1945 studierte er am Wagner College in Staten Island, New York, und kehrte 1948 für ein Aufbaustudium an der Escuela Nacional de Antropología e Historia (ENAH) nach Mexiko zurück. Seine Lehrer waren unter anderen Alfonso Caso, Paul Kirchhoff und José Pablo Martínez del Río. Mitte des Jahrhunderts kehrte er nach Österreich zurück, in jenes fast vergessene Land, um seine Doktorarbeit aus Völkerkunde an der Universität Wien zu schreiben und 1954 abzuschließen. Die Veröffentlichung seiner Dissertation zwei Jahre später kann als der Beginn seiner langen und erfolgreichen akademischen Karriere bezeichnet werden. Die Arbeit ist in Mexiko unter dem Titel *Situación social y económica de los aztecas durante los siglos XV y XVI* bekannt.[3] Sein Interesse an der prähispanischen Geschichte Lateinamerikas zeigte sich, als er im Jahr 1972 eine umfassende vergleichende Geschichte der Azteken, Maya und Inka mit dem Titel *The ancient American civilizations* veröffentlichte. Dieses Werk war drei Jahre zuvor in Deutschland unter dem Titel *Vorkolumbische Kulturen* veröffentlicht worden.[4]

1956 verließ Katz Wien, um eine Anstellung im Institut für Allgemeine Geschichte an der Humboldt-Universität in Ost-Berlin zu übernehmen und dort zwölf Jahre lang zu bleiben. Während seiner Arbeit an der Humboldt-Universität hatten sich seine Interessen von der Völkerkunde entfernt und auf die Geschichtswissenschaften ausgerichtet. Seine Habilitation verfasste Katz zur Neueren Geschichte Mexikos, konkret über die Beziehungen Mexikos zu Deutschland während des Porfiriats und der Revolution. Dieser Text erschien 1964 unter dem Titel *Deutschland, Diaz und die mexikanische Revolution*.[5] Katz hatte nicht nur das Thema und die Kollegen gewechselt,[6] seine Studien zur modernen Geschichte ermöglichten es ihm auch, sich nun aktuellen Problemen

[3] Katz, Friedrich: *Situación social y económica de los aztecas durante los siglos XV y XVI*, Universidad Nacional Autónoma de México (Instituto de Investigaciones Históricas), México, D.F. 1966.

[4] Katz, Friedrich: *The ancient American civilizations*, Praeger, New York u.a. 1972. Katz, Friedrich: *Vorkolumbische Kulturen. Die großen Reiche des alten Amerika*, Kindler, München 1969.

[5] Katz, Friedrich: *Deutschland, Diaz und die mexikanische Revolution. Die deutsche Politik in Mexiko 1870–1920* (=Schriftenreihe des Instituts für Allgemeine Geschichte an der Humboldt-Universität Berlin 9), Deutscher Verlag d. Wissenschaften, Berlin 1964.

[6] Die Gründe hierfür können Martina Kallers Beitrag zu diesem Band *Friedrich Katz an der Universität Wien. Von der Exzellenz ins Nichts* entnommen werden.

zuzuwenden. Außerdem konnte er die Außenpolitik Deutschlands studieren – ein Land, das er seit seiner Kindheit versucht hatte zu begreifen. Doch wie schon zuvor in seinem Leben musste Katz abermals aus politischen Gründen seinen Wohnsitz wechseln.

Katz wurde für das akademische Jahr 1968–1969 als Gastprofessor an die Universidad Nacional Autónoma de México (UNAM) eingeladen. Damit wurde er Zeuge der mexikanischen Variante der 1968er-Bewegung, während er gleichzeitig scharfe Kritik an der Repression gegen den demokratischen Aufbruch in der Tschechoslowakei übte. Kurz darauf, im Jahre 1970, blieb ihm nichts übrig als seine Stelle an der Humboldt-Universität in Ost-Berlin aufzugeben. Seine guten Verbindungen zu US-amerikanischen Kollegen machten sich bezahlt und er kehrte mit seiner Frau und den beiden Kindern in die Vereinigten Staaten zurück: zunächst für ein Jahr nach Austin, Texas, wo er eine Gastprofessur innehatte, dann nach Chicago, wo er den Rest seiner akademischen Laufbahn verbrachte.

Das Leben in den USA brachte einschneidende Veränderungen für Katz mit sich, die sich erneut auch in seiner akademischen Arbeit niederschlugen: Katz nahm eine zunehmend skeptische Haltung gegenüber dem Marxismus ein und gab seine Arbeit über die prähispanische Zeit auf, um sich ganz auf die Zeit der Mexikanischen Revolution zu konzentrieren. Mit *The Secret War in Mexico* fügte er 1981 der damals vorherrschenden Diplomatiegeschichte, die seine eigenen Veröffentlichungen aus der Berliner Zeit mit einschloss, eine neue Dimension hinzu. Seine neues, zweibändiges Werk war weder eine binäre Geschichte, in der Land gegen Land steht, noch beschränkte sie sich auf die Aktionen und Positionen von Außenministerien. Katz wählte eine mehrfache Perspektive, um die Komplexität der Politik der USA, Deutschlands, Großbritanniens und Frankreichs gegenüber der Mexikanischen Revolution zu analysieren. Neben den verschiedenen Regierungen untersuchte Katz auch revolutionäre Parteien, andere internationale Akteure und die Interessen von Unternehmen und Investoren, zum Beispiel von Ölgesellschaften, internationalen Banken oder Bürgen der mexikanischen Auslandsschulden. Auch militärhistorische Aspekte kamen darin vor. Summa summarum analysierte Katz die Mexikanische Revolution im globalen Kontext des Ersten Weltkriegs und trug damit entscheidend dazu bei, sie in der über die Fachwelt hinausgehenden Wahrnehmung als welthistorisches Ereignis zu etablieren.

The Secret War in Mexico thematisierte auch die Vorgeschichte der Revolution, so etwa die diplomatischen Beziehungen Mexikos während des Porfiriats.

Katz' Untersuchungen zu dieser Periode lassen sich auch in seinem Beitrag zur *Cambridge History of Latin America* nachlesen.[7] Zudem wurde ein Teil seiner Essays in zwei Sammelbänden veröffentlicht: *Ensayos Mexicanos* und *Nuevos Ensayos Mexicanos*.[8] 1998, beinahe zwanzig Jahre nach der Veröffentlichung von *The Secret War*, erschien fast gleichzeitig in englischer und spanischer Sprache seine Biographie über Pancho Villa, jenen Protagonisten der mexikanischen Heldenmythen, mit dem er seine Studien des modernen Mexiko begonnen hatte. Sein Wissen über Villa war unvergleichlich: Katz verstand die Gründe für den Aufstand in Nordmexiko, weil er sich mit der Region Chihuahua zur Zeit des Porfiriats gründlich auseinander gesetzt hatte und die Besonderheiten und Ziele dieses Kampfes zu analysieren vermochte. Er erkannte, was Villa antrieb, und kannte die Grenzen des gesellschaftspolitischen Projekts dieses Mannes aus dem Volk. Trotz seiner tiefen Sympathie für den Revolutionär wurde er kein Hagiograph Villas, sondern schrieb aus historisch-kritischer Distanz, wenn auch mit Empathie für seinen Gegenstand.

Dieses Werk geht weit über die Genregrenzen der Biographie hinaus: Es rekonstruiert nicht nur Villas Leben, sondern die damit verwobene Entwicklung der gesamten Villa-Bewegung. Außerdem räumt es auf mit all den Mythen und Legenden, Schwärmereien und Beleidigungen, Unwahrheiten und Halbwahrheiten, die sich um den Helden Pancho Villa ranken. Katz schrieb eine umfassende Geschichte der Mexikanischen Revolution mit Villa als einem der beiden Hauptakteure.[9] Mehr noch als eine historische Untersuchung war diese Arbeit eine Art detektivische Rekonstruktion: Katz folgte den Spuren, die Villa hinterlassen hatte. Der US-General John Pershing hatte den mexikanischen Revolutionär nicht dingfest machen können, doch Friedrich Katz gelang es. Er lieferte uns keinen toten Verbrecher, sondern einen lebendigen Revolutionär in all seiner Komplexität, seinen Widersprüchen und seiner Bedeutung für die Geschichte Mexikos.

Das Katz'sche Werk beschränkt sich jedoch nicht auf diese beiden großen Bücher, obwohl sie mehr als genug gewesen wären, um seinen Ruf als Historiker zu begründen. Sein drittes Interessensgebiet betraf die ungelösten Landkon-

---

[7] Katz, Friedrich: Mexico: Restored Republic and Porfiriato, 1867–1910, in: Bethell, Leslie (Hg.): *The Cambridge History of Latin America, Volume V: c. 1870 to 1930 (2)*, Cambridge University Press, Cambridge u.a. 1986, 3-78.

[8] Katz, Friedrich: *Ensayos Mexicanos*, Alianza, México, D.F. 1994. Katz, Friedrich: *Nuevos Ensayos Mexicanos*, ERA, México, D.F. 2006.

[9] John Womack analysierte 1969 die Geschichte der *Revolución del Sur* in: Womack, John: *Zapata and the Mexican Revolution*, Knopf, New York 1969.

flikte in der Geschichte Mexikos. Über dieses Thema schrieb er zwei wertvolle Beiträge. Beim ersten handelt es sich um eine Pionierarbeit, veröffentlicht im Jahr 1974 in der *Hispanic American Historical Review* unter dem Titel *Labor conditions on haciendas in Porfirian Mexico.*[10] Bereichert um wertvolle Quellenangaben erschien diese Arbeit im Jahre 1976 unter dem Titel *La servidumbre agraria en México en la época porfiriana* (*Die agrarische Knechtschaft in Mexiko im Porfiriat*).[11] Im Vergleich zu *The Secret War in Mexico* und *The Life and Times of Pancho Villa* ist diese Arbeit schlanker, ihr historiographischer Wert aber dennoch enorm. Katz entwarf eine historische Geographie des Landbesitzes und der unterschiedlichen Arbeitsverhältnisse, die jede Region und ihre je eigenen Eigentumsstrukturen hervorgebracht hatten. Seine Einteilung in drei große Zonen von Norden, Mitte und Süden Mexikos ermöglicht uns heute zu verstehen, worum es den sozialen Bewegungen während der Jahrzehnte der Revolution gegangen ist. Seinen zweiten Beitrag zu diesem Themengebiet lieferte er 1988 mit dem Buch *Riot, Rebellion, and Revolution: Rural social conflict in Mexico.*[12] Als Herausgeber dieses Sammelbandes und Autor der Einführung sowie zweier Kapitel zeigte Katz, dass das Hauptproblem der Geschichte Mexikos in der Struktur des Landbesitzes begründet ist. Er benennt damit die Ursachen für die bis heute andauernde Gewalt in der Gesellschaft. Sein Wissen über das, was in Mexiko am Land geschah und geschieht, erlaubte es ihm schließlich, eine Sozialgeschichte der Mexikanischen Revolution zu verfassen. In der Tat liegt der größte Unterschied zwischen *The Secret War in Mexico* und der Biographie über Pancho Villa im Wandel seiner Schwerpunktsetzung von der Diplomatie- zur Sozialgeschichte. Er wandte sich von Außenministern, Botschaftern und kosmopolitischen Hauptstädten ab und den rebellischen Bauern und am Rand lebenden Menschen Mexikos zu.

Von jenen Aspekten, die im Werk von Friedrich Katz besonders hervorragen, ist zunächst die internationale Dimension zu nennen: Katz hat aus der Mexikanischen Revolution ein Thema von globaler Relevanz gemacht und analysierte Villa aus vierfacher Perspektive: lokal, regional, national und inter-

---

[10] Katz, Friedrich: Labor conditions on haciendas in Porfirian Mexico: Some Trends and Tendencies, in: *The Hispanic American Historical Review* 54/1 (Februar 1974), 1-47.

[11] Katz, Friedrich (Hg.): *La servidumbre agraria en México en la época porfiriana* (=SepSetentas Bd. 303), Secretaría de Educación Pública, México, D.F. 1976.

[12] Katz, Friedrich (Hg.): *Riot, Rebellion, and Revolution: Rural social conflict in Mexico*, Princeton University Press, Princeton u.a. 1988. Die mexikanische Ausgabe erschien zwei Jahre später: Katz, Friedrich (Hg.): *Revuelta, rebelión y revolución: la lucha rural en México del siglo XVI al siglo XX*, 2 Bde., ERA, México, D.F. 1990.

national. Zweitens gelang es ihm, mit vergleichenden Methoden die Mexikanische Revolution und andere revolutionäre Bewegungen weltweit zueinander in Beziehung zu setzen. Er verglich auch Villa mit anderen mexikanischen Revolutionären, zum Beispiel Emiliano Zapata, und fand Schnittstellen zu weiteren Rebellen der Weltgeschichte. Der dritte Aspekt ist sein unverbrüchliches Engagement für Mexiko. Für Katz war die Geschichte unseres Landes mehr als ein bloß akademisches Interesse: Er fühlte sich dem Land verpflichtet, das ihm und seiner Familie in seinen Jugendtagen Zuflucht gewährt hatte.

Abschließend sei eine Facette angesprochen, die nur den wenigen bekannt ist, die seine Schüler sein durften: seine Meisterschaft als Dozent. Katz war ein großer Historiker und ein außergewöhnlicher Lehrer. Meine Erinnerungen gehen zurück bis in die späten 1970er Jahre. Obwohl ich wie Hunderte andere Studenten seine drei Semester währende Vorlesung „Latin American Civilization" besuchte, lernte ich ihn erst in seinem Dissertantenseminar über die Mexikanische Revolution kennen. Ich nahm teil, so oft ich konnte, und bewahre an all diese Seminare eine deutliche Erinnerung: Katz war ein mitreissender Vortragender, der stets perfekt vorbereitet war und nie bloß vortrug, sondern erklärte. Dank seiner weiten historischen Perspektive und analytischen Brillanz hat er uns jedes historische Problem, wie komplex es auch sein mochte, verständlich gemacht. Hinzu kam die komparatistische Schulung, verknüpfte und verglich Professor Katz doch Aspekte der Mexikanischen Revolution mit anderen Momenten der mexikanischen oder lateinamerikanischen Geschichte sowie mit anderen historischen Revolutionen, etwa der Französischen, Russischen oder Kubanischen Revolution. Seine Seminare über die Mexikanische Revolution gerieten so zum Anschauungsunterricht über Welt-, heute würde man sagen, Globalgeschichte.

Auch als sich sein Gesundheitszustand ernstlich verschlechterte, arbeitete Katz an mehreren Themen zugleich: über die *Científicos* der Periode von Porfirio Díaz, über die Familie Madero und über den militärischen Aufstand im Februar 1913. Leider blieb ihm nicht mehr die Zeit, um diesen Fragen in der gewohnten quellenkritischen Tiefe und analytischen Strenge nachzugehen. Und doch hinterließ er uns einen letzten Beweis seiner analytischen Meisterschaft: das posthum erschienene Buch *El Porfiriato y la Revolución en la historia de México* (*Das Porfiriat und die Revolution in der Geschichte Mexikos*).[13] Darin spiegelt sich einmal mehr das Interesse von Friedrich Katz an der Zeit von Díaz

[13] Katz, Friedrich/Lomnitz, Claudio: *El Porfiriato y la Revolución en la historia de México. Una conversación*, ERA, México, D.F. 2011.

und Madero. Sieben seiner neun Kapitel sind diesem Zeitabschnitt gewidmet. Das Buch ist das Produkt eines intellektuellen Dialogs mit seinem Schüler, Kollegen und Freund Claudio Lomnitz. Diese Gespräche fanden in den letzten Monaten seines Lebens statt und zeigen eine andere Seite von Katz. Er war dank seiner Geisteskraft und einer Kultur, die das Persönliche mit dem Allgemeinen in Zeit und Raum zu verbinden verstand, ein großartiger Redner. Seine Bücher hat er nicht geschrieben, sondern diktiert. An Stelle von Manuskripten befinden sich im Katz-Archiv denn auch Hunderte Tonbänder, die von seiner brillanten Rhetorik zeugen.

Friedrich Katz wurden viele Preise und Auszeichnungen zuteil: 1988 erhielt er in Mexiko den *Orden del Águila Azteca* verliehen, die höchste Auszeichnung der mexikanischen Regierung an Ausländer, die Großes für das Land geleistet haben. Kurz darauf ernannte ihn die Regierung des Bundesstaates Chihuahua zum Ehrenbürger und schließlich trägt das Center for Mexican Studies der University of Chicago seit 2004 seinen Namen. Mehrere Universitäten verliehen ihm ihr Ehrendoktorat. Andere Formen der Anerkennung sind freilich ebenso bedeutend: die Freundschaft vieler Mexikaner, der Respekt und die Bewunderung seiner Kollegen, die Zuneigung seiner Studenten und die Aufmerksamkeit seiner zahlreichen Leser. Seine Liebe zu Mexiko war unerschütterlich und schloss auch das Colegio de México ein: Friedrich Katz vermachte uns seine Bibliothek und beschenkte damit eine Forschungs- und Bildungseinrichtung Mexikos, die im Jahr 1940 von Präsident Lázaro Cárdenas für die *trasterrados*, die aus Spanien vertriebenen Intellektuellen in Mexiko, gegründet worden war. Möge sein Andenken für immer bewahrt sein und so auch der Dank seiner Kollegen, Studenten und Leser.

Wie wir in Mexiko zu sagen pflegen: „¡Lo vamos a querer siempre!“ Er wird uns unvergesslich bleiben!

Friedrich Katz: Versatile historian and Mexican by adoption

Javier Garciadiego

Friedrich Katz, who died on October 16, 2010, belonged to that rare breed of historians with a truly global reputation. He had to his credit two genuine classics of the historiography of the Mexican Revolution: *The Secret War in Mexico*[1] and *The Life and Times of Pancho Villa.*[2] From the countless instances of worldwide recognition of his academic work let me mention only the very last one, his nomination as Honorary President of the XIIIth Conference of Mexican, US, and Canadian Historians, held at Querétaro in October 2010. Though he accepted this honour with his usual humility his poor health prevented him from taking part in the conference. In the event he was to die ten days before it opened. Friedrich Katz' life matched the cosmopolitanism of the diplomatic history that underlies his view of the Mexican Revolution. Nowhere is this more evident that in his empathetic biography of Pancho Villa, whose turbulent childhood and early youth mirrored his own and for whom he had a great deal of admiration.

Friedrich Katz came from Vienna. His journalist father, Leo Katz, had been critical of Hitler and the Nazis, so when Hitler rose to power in Germany in 1933, the family fled to France, only to be expelled at the beginning of World War II. The parents and their only son moved to New York. As their tourist visa expired after a year and a return to Europe would have been life threatening for them, they had to seek refuge somewhere else. In 1940 they arrived in Mexico, where on the initiative of President Lázaro Cárdenas numerous political exiles from Central Europe and Spain were being granted asylum. Friedrich Katz was thirteen at the time. His life up that point was marked by persecution and rejection for reasons he was unable to understand. In addition to his German mother tongue he had picked up two more languages in the course of these few, intense years; at the French-Mexican school in Mexico he added a fourth, Spanish.

---

[1] Katz, Friedrich: *The Secret War in Mexico. Europe, the United States and the Mexican revolution*, University of Chicago Press, Chicago et al. 1981. Katz, Friedrich: *La Guerra Secreta en México*, 2 vols., ERA, México, D.F. 1982.

[2] Katz, Friedrich: *The Life and Times of Pancho Villa*, Stanford University Press, Stanford 1998. Katz, Friedrich: *Pancho Villa*, 2 vols., ERA, México, D.F. 1998.

Friedl, as his German-speaking friends used to call him, acquired the rudiments of Mexican history at home rather than at school and it proved to be a topic that he took to heart from the very beginning. From 1945 he was a student at Wagner College in Staten Island, New York, returning in 1948 to the Escuela Nacional de Antropología e Historia (ENAH) in Mexico for a postgraduate course. His teachers included Alfonso Caso, Paul Kirchhoff and José Pablo Martínez del Río. In the late 1940s he returned to Austria, a country he had already largely forgotten, in order to write his doctoral thesis in ethnology at the University of Vienna; he graduated in 1954. The publication of his PhD thesis two years later may be considered the true beginning of his long and highly successful academic career. The thesis has become a standard work in Mexico under the title *Situación social y económica de los aztecas durante los siglos XV y XVI.*[3] Katz' interest in the pre-Hispanic history of Latin America can also be seen in a comprehensive comparative history of the Aztecs, Mayas and Incas, *The ancient American civilizations*, which was published in 1972. This work had appeared in Germany three years earlier under the title *Vorkolumbische Kulturen.*[4]

In 1956 Katz left Vienna to take up a post at the Department of History in the Humboldt University in East Berlin, where he was to remain for twelve years. During his time at the Humboldt University his interest shifted away from ethnology and towards history. For his habilitation Katz chose a topic from Mexico's modern history: the relationship between Mexico and Germany during the Porfiriato and the Revolution. The work was published in 1964 under the title *Deutschland, Diaz und die mexikanische Revolution.*[5] Katz had not only supplied himself with a new theme, he had also moved on to a new set of colleagues[6] and his new-found interest in modern history enabled him to turn his

---

[3] Katz, Friedrich: *Situación social y económica de los aztecas durante los siglos XV y XVI*, Universidad Nacional Autónoma de México (Instituto de Investigaciones Históricas), México, D.F. 1966.

[4] Katz, Friedrich: *The ancient American civilizations*, Praeger, New York et al. 1972. Katz, Friedrich: *Vorkolumbische Kulturen. Die großen Reiche des alten Amerika*, Kindler, München 1969.

[5] Katz, Friedrich: *Deutschland, Diaz und die mexikanische Revolution. Die deutsche Politik in Mexiko 1870–1920* (=Schriftenreihe des Instituts für Allgemeine Geschichte an der Humboldt-Universität Berlin 9), Deutscher Verlag d. Wissenschaften, Berlin 1964.

[6] The reasons for this are to be found in Martina Kaller's contribution to this volume *Friedrich Katz an der Universität Wien. Von der Exzellenz ins Nichts* [*Friedrich Katz at the University of Vienna. From excellence to nothingness*].

attention to present-day problems. It enabled him moreover to study the foreign policy of Germany, a country he had wanted to get to grips with from his childhood. The next step he had to take was one he had already gone through several times in his life: political conditions, this time in the GDR of the late 1960s, forced him to move to another country.

Katz was invited to the Universidad Nacional Autónoma de México (UNAM) as a visiting professor for the academic year 1968–1969. This allowed him to become a witness to the Mexican variant of the movement of 1968 and provided a platform for his vehement criticism of the way the democratic movement was stifled in Czechoslovakia. He then had no choice but to give up his post at the Humboldt University in East Berlin in 1970. His excellent connections with colleagues in the USA helped pave the way for his return to the United States with his wife and two children, initially to Austin, Texas, for a year as a visiting professor, and then to Chicago, where he spent the rest of his academic career.

Life in the United States brought decisive changes for Katz, as can be seen quite clearly in his academic work: his attitude towards Marxism became increasingly sceptical and he abandoned his work on the pre-Hispanic era to concentrate all his energy on the time of the Mexican Revolution. In *The Secret War in Mexico* (1981) he added an entirely new dimension to the then prevailing strain of diplomatic history, which included his own publications from his time in Berlin. This two-volume work was neither binary in the sense of pitting two countries against one another nor did it confine itself to the actions and positions taken by foreign ministries. Katz opted for a multiple perspective in the hope that this would allow him to analyze more fully the complexity of the policies of the United States, Germany, Great Britain and France towards the Mexican Revolution. In addition to the different governments, the objects of Katz' analysis included revolutionary parties and other international agents and the interests of corporations and investors such as oil companies, banks and the guarantors of Mexico's foreign debt. It also dealt with aspects of military history. Broadly speaking, Katz analyzed the Mexican Revolution in the global context of World War I and it is largely thanks to him and his work that Mexico's revolution is now perceived as an event of world-historical significance, potentially of as much interest to the general public as to circles of specialists.

The Secret War in Mexico also addressed the prehistory of the Revolution, including Mexico's diplomatic standing during the Porfiriato. Katz' analyses of issues relevant to that time are also included in his contributions to the

Cambridge History of Latin America.[7] Two volumes, *Ensayos Mexicanos* and *Nuevos Ensayos Mexicanos*,[8] pull together many of his essays. In 1998, nearly twenty years after the publication of *The Secret War*, Katz' biography of Pancho Villa, the foremost protagonist of Mexican heroic myths, was published almost simultaneously in English and Spanish. His expertise on Villa defies comparison. The intimate knowledge of what life in the Chihuahua region was like in the days of the Porfiriato and of the special characteristics and aims of the struggle gave Katz a unique vantage point in his effort to understand the causes of the rebellion in Northern Mexico. He knew what motivated Villa and was equally aware of the limitations of the socio-political project conceived by this man of the people. Katz' deeply felt sympathies for this revolutionary did not make him his hagiographer and the empathy with which he treated his subject merely lends additional lustre to his historical and critical detachment.

It may justly be said of this work that it far transcends the genre boundaries of biography: it is a reconstruction not only of Villa's life but of the whole movement of which that life was a part. It disposes of the myths and legends, of the flattering or pejorative accretions, of the lies and half-truths that had become associated with the heroic Pancho Villa. What Katz has given us is a comprehensive history of the Mexican Revolution with Villa one of two protagonists.[9] It is a heavily contextualized biography and a kind of historical paper chase. Katz picks up the trail left by Villa and succeeds where the US General John Pershing had failed. He delivers us not a dead criminal but a living being, a revolutionary complete with all his complexity, his contradictions and, above all, his significance for Mexico's history.

Great though these two works are and more than sufficient to put his reputation as a historian beyond dispute, Katz' oeuvre and his claim to fame do not rest exclusively on them. His third area of interest was the unresolved land conflict, a perennial theme of Mexican history, to which he made two valuable contributions. The first is a pioneering study published in 1974 in the *Hispanic American Historical Review* under the title *Labor conditions on haciendas in*

---

[7] Katz, Friedrich: Mexico: Restored Republic and Porfiriato, 1867–1910, in: Bethell, Leslie (ed.): *The Cambridge History of Latin America, Volume V: c. 1870 to 1930 (2)*, Cambridge University Press, Cambridge et al. 1986, 3-78.

[8] Katz, Friedrich: *Ensayos Mexicanos*, Alianza, México, D.F. 1994. Katz, Friedrich: *Nuevos Ensayos Mexicanos*, ERA, México, D.F. 2006.

[9] 1969 saw the publication of John Womack's analysis of the *Revolución del Sur* in: Womack, John: *Zapata and the Mexican Revolution*, Knopf, New York 1969.

Porfirian Mexico.[10] Enlarged and now containing additional valuable source material, it appeared in book form in 1976 entitled *La servidumbre agraria en México en la época porfiriana* (*The Agrarian Servitude in Mexico During the Porfirian Years*).[11] Compared with *The Secret War in Mexico* and *The Life and Times of Pancho Villa* this is a slim work but in historiographical terms its impact was nevertheless enormous. Katz outlined a historical geography of land ownership and the labour relations that differed in each region according to their specific structures of ownership. The way he splits his focus on Mexico into three zones, North, Centre and South, enables us to understand what aims the different social movements were pursuing over the two decades of the revolution. His second great contribution to this theme was *Riot, Rebellion, and Revolution: Rural social conflict in Mexico* (1988).[12] As the editor of this volume and author of the introduction and two of its chapters, Katz demonstrates that the chief problem hampering Mexico throughout its history has been the structure of land ownership, thereby putting his finger on the cause of the violence that persists to this day. It was his detailed knowledge of what had happened and was still happening in his time in rural Mexico that enabled him to write his social history of the Mexican Revolution. The most important difference between *The Secret War in Mexico* and the biography of Pancho Villa lies in the shift of the focus from diplomatic to social history. He turned away from ministers, ambassadors and cosmopolitan venues to rebellious farmers and people living at the margins of Mexican society.

From among the aspects of the oeuvre of Friedrich Katz that make it so outstanding let me mention first of all the international dimension: Katz has turned the Mexican Revolution into a topic of global relevance. His analyses, of which Villa is an excellent example, typically span four dimensions: local, regional, national and international. Secondly, he successfully employed comparative means to establish relationships between the Mexican Revolution and other revolutionary movements elsewhere in the world. At the same time he compared Villa with other Mexican revolutionaries, such as Emiliano Zapata,

---

[10] Katz, Friedrich: Labor conditions on haciendas in Porfirian Mexico: Some Trends and Tendencies, in: *The Hispanic American Historical Review* 54/1 (February 1974), 1-47.

[11] Katz, Friedrich (ed.): *La servidumbre agraria en México en la época porfiriana* (=SepSetentas vol. 303), Secretaría de Educación Pública, México, D.F. 1976.

[12] Katz, Friedrich (ed.): *Riot, Rebellion, and Revolution: Rural social conflict in Mexico*, Princeton University Press, Princeton et al. 1988. The Mexican edition was published two years later: Katz, Friedrich (ed.): *Revuelta, rebelión y revolución: la lucha rural en México del siglo XVI al siglo XX*, 2 vols., ERA, México, D.F. 1990.

and identified a number of traits that Villa had in common with rebels from world history. The third aspect was his unfailing commitment to Mexico. For Katz the history of our country was not an object of mere academic curiosity: he maintained strong emotional ties to Mexico, which had been a place of refuge for him and his family in the days of his youth.

Finally let me mention a facet of Katz that only those few who have had the privilege of being his students are familiar with: his skills as a teacher. Katz was a great historian *and* an outstanding teacher. My memories of him go back to the late 1970s. I had been one of several hundred students who attended his three-term lecture "Latin American Civilization" and did not really get to know him well until I became a member of his PhD seminar on the Mexican Revolution. I took part in as many sessions as possible and have very clear memories of them. Katz was a brilliant lecturer, who was always impeccably prepared; he never simply delivered his lecture but took great pains to explain anything he felt needed explaining; his sweeping historical perspective and his analytical skills were such that he succeeded in making historical developments intelligible, no matter how complex they were. His comparative approach enabled him to link aspects of the Mexican Revolution to other crucial moments in Mexican or Latin American history and to revolutionary processes such as the French, Russian and Cuban Revolutions. This turned his seminars on the Mexican Revolution into what one might call forays into global history.

His failing health towards the end of his life did not deter Katz from working simultaneously on several themes, including the *Científicos* in the era of Porfirio Díaz, the Madero family and the military uprising in February 1913. Unfortunately he simply ran out of time and was no longer permitted to pursue his themes with the analytical rigour and the untiring attention to the sources that were his hallmark. Nevertheless, *El Porfiriato y la Revolución en la historia de México*,[13] which was published after Katz' death, shows him still in full possession of his analytical powers. It mirrors once more his interest in the time of Díaz and Madero: seven of its nine chapters are devoted to topics related to this epoch. The book is the result of a dialogue between Katz and his student, colleague and friend Claudio Lomnitz, which took place in the last months of his life and reveals yet another side of Katz. His superb intellectual powers and his cultural background, which enabled him to link personal to general considerations reaching out in space and time, made him an accomplished rhetorician.

[13] Katz, Friedrich/Lomnitz, Claudio: *El Porfiriato y la Revolución en la historia de México. Una conversación*, ERA, México, D.F. 2011.

Instead of writing his books he dictated them and instead of manuscripts there are hundreds of recorded tapes in the Katz Archive that document his brilliant rhetorical gifts.

Friedrich Katz received numerous prizes and distinctions: in 1988 Mexico awarded him the Order of the Aztec Eagle, the *Orden del Águila Azteca*, the Mexican government's highest decoration for foreigners of outstanding merit. Shortly afterwards he was made an honorary citizen of Chihuahua, the largest of Mexico's thirty-one states, and last but not least the Center for Mexican Studies of the University of Chicago was named after him in 2004. Several universities have awarded him honorary doctorates. Other forms of recognition, which are at least as important, are the friendly feelings many Mexicans harbour towards him, the respect and admiration of his colleagues, the grateful memories that his students have of him and the loyalty of his numerous readers. His unceasing love of Mexico also extended to the Colegio de México: Friedrich Katz left his books to us, making a generous gift to a Mexican research and educational institution founded in 1940 by President Lázaro Cárdenas for the *trasterrados*, the intellectuals ousted from Spain who had found refuge in Mexico. May his memory live forever in the gratitude of his colleagues, students and readers.

As we are wont to say in Mexico: "¡Lo vamos a querer siempre!" We will always miss him.

Friedrich Katz an der Universität Wien. Von der Exzellenz ins Nichts

Martina Kaller

Welche Rolle spielen Wien und die Universität Wien im Leben des Friedrich Katz?[1] Bekannt ist, dass Katz in Wien 1927 geboren wurde und hier seine ersten drei Lebensjahre verbrachte. Bekannt dürfte auch sein, dass Katz Ende der 1940er Jahre mit seiner Familie nach Wien zurückkehrte und an der Universität Wien sein Doktoratsstudium absolvierte. Auch nachdem er Wien 1956 wieder verlassen hatte, spielte die Stadt – kaum jedoch die Universität Wien – in späteren Jahrzehnten immer wieder eine Rolle im Leben von Friedrich Katz. Den vielfältigen historischen Spuren, welche die Familie Katz in Wien hinterließ, gilt es in Zukunft noch nachzugehen. Im Folgenden sei eine erste Sondierung in Bezug auf Friedrich Katz und die Universität Wien versucht.

Im Archiv der Universität Wien befinden sich drei Akten, die Friedrich Katz betreffen: 1.) sein Inskriptionsblatt (die so genannte „Nationale") von 1949 bis 1954;[2] 2.) sein Rigorosenakt[3] und 3.) sein Stammdatenblatt,[4] das ihn im Sommersemester 1981 als Gastprofessor am Institut für Geschichte ausweist. Ferner gibt es das Protokoll von einer Berufungskommission zur Besetzung des „Lehrstuhl für Außereuropäische Geschichte unter besonderer Berücksichtigung Lateinamerikas", also der einzigen Professur an einer österreichischen Hochschule für die Geschichte Lateinamerikas. Friedrich Katz, der ursprünglich für diese, Anfang der 1980er Jahre neu geschaffene Stelle gewonnen werden sollte, wusste in Kenntnis der akademischen Praxis in den USA um die Wichtigkeit solcher auf bestimmte Fragen und Regionen fokussierter Professuren. Sie erlauben es, ein amerikanistisches Forschungs- und Lehrprofil zu entwickeln, das im Fach international ausstrahlen könnte.

Bevor ich chronologisch fortfahre, möchte ich anmerken, dass ich erst seit 1989 Zeugin der Geschichte um den „Friedrich-Katz-Lehrstuhl" – so könnte er

---

[1] Ich danke Herrn Kollegen Gernot Heiß für seine unverzichtbare Unterstützung bei meinen Recherchen zu diesem Beitrag.

[2] Archiv der Universität Wien, Inskriptionsblatt /„Nationale", Philosophische Fakultät, Nationale WS 1949/50 (alphabethisch eingeordnet).

[3] Archiv der Universität Wien, Rigorosenakt 18.955, Friedrich Katz, 26.01.1954 bis 22.12.1954.

[4] Archiv der Universität Wien, Personalakt 4390, Friedrich Katz (1981) K 525.

heißen – bin. Alle früheren Ereignisse können aus Archivmaterial rekonstruiert werden. So kenne ich denn auch die Kommission zur Besetzung einer Gastprofessur und die erste Berufungskommission zur Besetzung des Lehrstuhls für „Außereuropäische Geschichte mit besonderer Berücksichtigung Lateinamerikas" nur aus den Protokollen. Diese war nach einer zweiten Ausschreibung erfolgreich: 1990 wurde der Lehrstuhl mit Gerhard Drekonja besetzt. Ich bin seit seiner Emeritierung vor fünf Jahren bis dato als einzige habilitierte Assistentin in diesem Fachbereich verblieben. Die bisherigen Versuche mit zwei Ausschreibungen (und einer Berufungskommission in unterschiedlicher Besetzung), diese Professur nachzubesetzen, sind gescheitert, nicht zuletzt aufgrund der halbherzigen Berufungs- und Einladungspraxis. Diese im deutschen Sprachraum so rare lateinamerikabezogene Professur ist also weiterhin vakant – ein gerade in diesen Tagen bedauerlicher Umstand, denn der Internationale Amerikanistenkongress (ICA) tagt im Sommer 2012 zum dritten Mal in Wien (zuvor bereits 1908 und 1960) und zum ersten Mal an der Universität Wien.

Der erste der drei großen *round tables*, die am 54. ICA in Wien abgehalten werden, ist Friedrich Katz gewidmet. Als Präsidentin des 54. ICA ist es mir eine Ehre, zusammen mit den KollegInnen vom *Katz-Center for Mexican Studies* an der University of Chicago und den Kollegen am Colegio de México diese Sitzung zu eröffnen und gerade in jener Stadt dem Doyen der Geschichte Mexikos ein Andenken zu widmen, die Katz selbst für den grundlegenden Bezugsort in seinem Leben hielt. Seinem Wunsch gemäß fand Friedrich Katz, der am 16. Oktober 2010 in Philadelphia verstarb, am Wiener Zentralfriedhof seine letzte Ruhestätte.

Friedrich Katz hatte mehrmals versucht, nach Wien zurückzukehren. Er selbst meinte im Gespräch, er sei zweimal aus Österreich vertrieben worden. Zum ersten Mal als Kind. Damit gehört er zur Gruppe der „Überleber", wie Ivan Illich (wörtlich aus dem Englischen) es nannte. Auch Illich war wie Katz ein aktiver Lebender, kein passiver Überlebender des Austrofaschismus und Nationalsozialismus. Illich ist nicht nach Österreich zurückgekehrt.[5] Seine „zweite", von Katz so bezeichnete, „Vertreibung", gedieh auf dem Nährboden der „zweimal verdrängten Vergangenheit" Österreichs: Vertreter der „klerikal-konservativen Restauration der Nachkriegszeit mit antisemitischem Subtext"[6] an der Universität Wien vermasselten ihm das Rigorosenzeugnis.

---

[5] Kaller-Dietrich, Martina: *Ivan Illich (1927–2002). Sein Leben, sein Denken*, Bibliothek der Provinz, Weitra/Wien 2008.

[6] Stadler, Friedrich: Philosophie – Zwischen „Anschluss" und Ausschluss, Restauration und Innovation, in: Grandner, Margarete/Heiss, Gernot/Rathkolb, Oliver (Hg.): *Zukunft mit Altlasten. Die Universität Wien 1945 bis 1955* (=Querschnitte 19), Studienverlag, Innsbruck u.a. 2005, 121-136, hier 131.

Studium an der Universität Wien: 1949 bis 1954

Friedrich Katz hatte Glück, denn seine Eltern, Bronia und Leo Katz, verließen Österreich 1933. Aus seinem Curriculum Vitae, das er im Jahr 1954 zusammen mit der Dissertationsschrift für seine Anmeldung zum Rigorosum abgab, geht folgendes hervor: Volkschule in Paris, Gymnasium in New York und anschliessend das Lycée Français in Mexiko Stadt. 1945 beendete er seine Schulkarriere eben dort. Nach einer weiteren Graduierung zum *Bachelor of Arts* in New York und einem einjährigen Aufenthalt an der renommierten Escuela Nacional de Antropología e Historia (ENAH) in Mexiko inskribierte Friedrich Katz an der Philosophischen Fakultät der Universität Wien das Studienfach Völkerkunde. Er war damals 22 Jahre alt und hatte die für einen Amerikanisten unerlässlichen Arbeitssprachen Französisch, Englisch und Spanisch im Gepäck. Damit war er im Schnitt älter als seine Kommilitonen und gewiss besser vorgebildet als die meisten anderen. Sein Studienbuch belegt seine guten Leistungen und zeigt nichts Auffallendes.

Sein Rigorosenakt hingegen schon:[7] Der Doktorvater Wilhelm Koppers würdigte die Dissertation von Friedrich Katz mit „sehr gut". Im Gutachten vom 22. Februar 1954 ist von „der derzeit besten Untersuchung der Soziologie der Azteken" die Rede. Eine Drucklegung wird empfohlen.

Pater Wilhelm Koppers (1886–1961) war enger Mitarbeiter von Pater Wilhelm Schmidt (1868–1954), dem Begründer der „Wiener Schule der Kulturkreislehre". In seinem Gutachten zur Dissertation von Friedrich Katz heißt es mit Kniefall vor dem Interessensschwerpunkt Schmidts: „Diese These [...] vermittelt auch interessante Ausblicke auf altweltliche Kulturen." Eben nur Aus- und keine Einblicke; denn Katz' Soziologie der Azteken des 15. und 16. Jahrhunderts ist eine Untersuchung über die wirtschaftlichen und gesellschaftlichen Verhältnisse im langen Jahrhundert der Erstkolonialisierung Mesoamerikas und folgt eindeutig einer historisch-materialistischen Grundausrichtung. Antievolutionistische Spekulationen über die Ein-Gott-Nähe der „primitivsten" Kulturen und von deren schriftloser Ausbreitung[8] (Diffusionslehre), wie Koppers es von Schmidt im Kreis der Societas Verbi Divini gelernt hatte, kommen nicht vor. Die Societas war ein Missionsorden mit Sitz in Freiburg in der Schweiz, St. Augustin bei Bonn und St. Gabriel in Mödling bei Wien. André Gingrich, 1993–2001 stellvertretender Institutsvorstand am Institut für Ethnologie, Kultur-

---

[7] AUW, Rigorosenakt Katz.

[8] Keine der fünf mesoamerikanischen Zivilisationen war schriftlos.

und Sozialanthropologie, bezeichnet die „Wiener Schule der Kulturkreislehre" als „geheimbündlerisches Netzwerk" mit „doktrinärer Disziplin", die im spätkolonialen und missionspolitischen Kontext zur „Stütze des Austrofaschismus und dessen Allianzen" (Mussolini) avanciert war.[9]

Knapp zwei Monate nachdem Koppers sein Gutachten verfasst hatte, setzte Robert Heine-Geldern seine Unterschrift darunter. Damit erklärte er sich mit der Note „sehr gut" von Koppers einverstanden. Heine-Geldern (1885–1968) war nach seiner Flucht aus Wien im Jahr 1938 der international anerkannteste unter den Wiener Diffusionisten. Während Koppers nach Kriegsende umgehend aus der Schweiz nach Wien zurückgekehrt war, um als „neuer alter" Ordinarius das Institut für Völkerkunde der Universität Wien zu leiten, musste Heine-Geldern bis Ende 1950 auf seine Ernennung zum „außerordentlichen Professor" warten. Er hatte noch in den USA verbleibend dafür gesorgt, dass die Wenner Gren Foundation for Anthropological Research (New York) 1946 die Burg Wartenstein bei Gloggnitz als Konferenzzentrum ankaufte.[10] Erst 1955 wurde Heine-Geldern Ordentlicher Professor, ein Rang, den er schon lange vor seiner Vertreibung innegehabt hatte.

Möglicherweise hatte Katz gehofft, in Wien *sub auspiciis Praesidentis* zu promovieren, wodurch ihm eine neue Assistentenstelle zugestanden wäre. Mit dem Philosophicum, dem zweiten großen Prüfungsfach seines Doktorrigorosums, das er am 4.12.1954 absolvierte, war Katz aber aus dem Spiel. Als Hauptprüfer trat Leo Gabriel (1902–1987) auf, damals Ordinarius für Philosophie. Er beurteilte Katz' Prüfungsleistung mit „genügend" (was aus Philosophie-Psychologie das „Hauptkalkül" „genügend" ergab). Es wurden damals keine Prüfungsprotokolle angelegt, weshalb über Inhalt und Verlauf der Prüfung nicht einmal Vermutungen angestellt werden können. Fest steht, dass Leo Gabriel als seit 1947 Habilitierter mit seiner Ganzheitsphilosophie und seiner „integralen Logik" jahrzehntelang für die Kontinuität des politischen Katholizismus am Institut für Philosophie der Universität Wien sorgte. Zusammen mit Erich Heintl (1912–2000) stand Gabriel für die Verbannung von Marxismus und Positivismus als „Labyrinthe der Philosophie" aus der Lehre. Diese Fortschreibung der Ideologie des Ständestaats verhinderte auch die Remigration und die akademische Etablierung jener vertriebenen Philosophen an der Universität Wien.[11]

---

[9] Gingrich, Andre: Remigranten und Ehemalige: Zäsuren und Kontinuitäten in der universitären Völkerkunde Wiens nach 1945, in: Grandner, Margarete/Heiss, Gernot/Rathkolb, Oliver (Hg.): *Zukunft mit Altlasten. Die Universität Wien 1945 bis 1955* (=Querschnitte 19), Studienverlag, Innsbruck u.a. 2005, 260-272, hier 263.

[10] Gingrich, Remigranten, 264-266.

[11] Stadler, Philosophie, 134.

1954 war Friedrich Katz in doppelter Hinsicht an der Philosophischen Fakultät der Universität Wien nicht erwünscht: Was Katz, der damals KP-Mitglied war, in die DDR gehen ließ, kann ich mir zumindest vorstellen. Belege gibt es für diese Entscheidung keine. Er hat einmal erzählt, dass Anna Seghers, die er aus der Emigration in Mexiko kannte, ihm dabei behilflich war.

Zwei Jahre schlug sich Friedrich Katz mehr schlecht als recht mit einem mageren Lohn als Journalist der kommunistischen Tageszeitung *Der Abend* durch,[12] bis er mit einer Assistentenstelle an der Humboldt-Universität zu Berlin ab 1956 eine neue wissenschaftliche Arbeitsstätte fand. In der Zwischenzeit hatte der erwähnte Heine-Geldern nach seiner Emeritierung 1960 in Wien am Völkerkundemuseum die Präsidentschaft des XXXIV. ICA übernommen. Nach heutiger Nomenklatur handelte es sich um den 34. ICA. Die gedruckte Dokumentation des Kongresses füllt 854 Seiten. Neuerungen im ICA als internationalem Zusammenschluss der AmerikanistInnen waren im Juli 1960 in Wien nicht zu vermerken.[13] Friedrich Katz wird zusammen mit Walter Markov aus Leipzig als Mitglied verzeichnet, nicht aber im Autorenverzeichnis der Akten gelistet (Walter Markov betreute die Habilitation von Katz an der Humboldt-Universität). Wie aus verschiedenen Erwähnungen im Personalakt Katz' an der Humboldt-Universität hervorgeht, war Katz beim 34. ICA anwesend.[14] Als einziger aus der DDR kommender Autor mit Beitrag scheint in den Akten allerdings der Leipziger Manfred Kossok auf.[15]

---

[12] Vgl. die Angaben zur vorangehenden beruflichen Tätigkeiten in: Universitätsarchiv der Humboldt-Universität zu Berlin, Personalakte K 1102, Prof. Dr. Friedrich Katz (=UA HUB Personalakt Katz), Personalbogen.

[13] *Akten des 34. Internationalen Amerikanistenkongresses. Wien, 18.–25. Juli 1960*, Verlag Ferdinand Berger, Horn/Wien 1962. Comas, Juan: *Cien años de Congresos Internacionales de Americanistas. Ensayo histórico-crítico y bibliográfico*, Instituto de Investigaciones Históricas/Instituto de Investigaciones Antropológicas de la UNAM, México, D.F. 1974. Comas geht nur auf jene ICAs ein, bei denen innovative Schritte im Hinblick auf den internationalen Amerikanismus gesetzt wurden. Der 34. ICA wird nicht näher erläutert. Eine der Innovationen am 54. ICA in Wien besteht darin, dass es erstmals unter dem Vorsitz von Josefina Echavarría Álvarez einen Themenschwerpunkt zu Gender Studies geben wird.

[14] Vgl. verschiedene Gutachten und Briefe, welche die Teilnahme Katz' erwähnen in: UA HUB Personalakt Katz.

[15] Kossoks Beitrag erschien unter dem Titel *Buenos Aires und die Genesis des Kolonialbürgertums im La Plata-Gebiet*, in: *Akten des 34. Internationalen Amerikanistenkongresses. Wien, 18.–25. Juli 1960*, Verlag Ferdinand Berger, Horn/Wien 1962, 814-825.
Da Österreich die DDR erst später (1975) anerkannte, werden Katz, Kossok und Markov auch in den Kongress-Akten des 34. ICA nicht unter „Delegierte von Universitäten, wis-

Berlin und Ruf nach Wien

Von 1956 bis 1963 war Friedrich Katz an der Humboldt Universität zu Berlin als Assistent tätig, von 1963 bis 1966 als Dozent und von 1966 bis 1970 als Professor (ab 1969 als „ordentlicher Professor"). Die „sehr gute" Dissertation von Friedrich Katz erschien 1956 in der DDR unter dem Titel *Die sozialökonomischen Verhältnisse bei den Azteken im 15. und 16. Jahrhundert* im Deutschen Verlag der Wissenschaften, Berlin. Nur sechs Jahre danach habilitierte sich Katz am 28. November 1962 an der Humboldt Universität zu Berlin mit seiner ersten transatlantischen Diplomatiegeschichte: *Deutschland, Diaz und die mexikanische Revolution: Die deutsche Politik in Mexiko 1870–1920*. Sein wissenschaftlicher Werdegang setzte sich nach seinem Protest gegen den Einmarsch der Warschauer-Pakt-Truppen in Prag im Jahr 1968 glücklich in den Amerikas fort: Erst verbrachte er das Wintersemester 1968, überschattet vom Massaker auf der *Plaza de las Tres Culturas* am 2. Oktober 1968, das als *Noche de Tlatelolco* in die Geschichte eingegangen ist, am Institut für Politikwissenschaften der Universidad Nacional Autónoma de México (UNAM). 1970 las er als Gastprofessor an der University of Austin und 1971 erhielt er den Ruf als *Professor of Latin American History* an die University of Chicago. Die Entscheidung nach den wilden 1968ern zugunsten des Kommunisten und Antiimperialisten Friedrich Katz kann als Antwort auf die Berufung von John Womack[16] auf einen gleichnamigen Lehrstuhl in Harvard gelesen werden.

Von Chicago kam Katz im Jahr 1981 als Gastprofessor für „Neuere Außereuropäische Geschichte – Lateinamerika" nach Wien. In der Bestellung steht, dass Katz mit einem zweistündigen Seminar am Institut für Völkerkunde (damals bereits nicht mehr an der Philosophischen, sondern an der Grund- und Integrativwissenschaftlichen Fakultät angesiedelt) einen Teil der Lehre von

senschaftlichen Instituten und Gesellschaften" genannt. Vgl. Akten 34. ICA, 12-16. Zu den Beziehungen zwischen Katz, Markov und Kossok im Rahmen der Lateinamerikaforschung in der DDR siehe auch den Beitrag von David Mayer in diesem Band *Der Weltenläufer: Friedrich Katz und die historiographischen Debatten seiner Zeit.*

[16] John Womack Jr. hat in Harvard studiert und mit Auszeichnung promoviert. Dies sicherte dem Autor des zum damaligen Zeitpunkt wichtigsten historischen Werks zur Mexikanischen Revolution (*Zapata and the Mexican Revolution*, 1969) eine Anstellung als Professor für lateinamerikanische Geschichte an seiner Alma Mater. Am 24.11.2009 emeritierte Womack. Drei Tage zuvor erhielt er von der Regierung von Mexiko-Stadt für seine Verdienste um Mexiko die „1808"-Medaille überreicht. Diesen Orden schenkte er den mutigen Gewerkschaftern der mexikanischen Elektrizitätswerke. Siehe dazu: *La Jornada*, 21.11.2009, 17.

Walter Dostal, seinem ehemaligen Studienkollegen und Spezialisten für den Vorderen Orient, übernehmen sollte, was auch geschah. Dass diese Gastprofessur am Institut für Geschichte (IfG) und nicht am Institut für Völkerkunde oder Zeitgeschichte eingerichtet wurde, hatte der damalige Vorstand am IfG, Gerald Stourzh, erreicht. Dieser betrieb auch maßgeblich die Anwerbung von Katz als Ordinarius an die Universität Wien. Als es 1983 soweit war, sagte Friedrich Katz ab. Er führte private Gründe ins Treffen. Die ungewöhnlich hohe Abwehrdotation für ihn vonseiten der University of Chicago dürfte ihm die Entscheidung erleichtert haben.[17]

So, wie ich mich an ihn erinnere, war es wohl weniger das Geld als die damit verbundene hohe Anerkennung seiner Leistungen in jenem Land, in welchem ihm zweimal aus der existenziellen Bedrängnis geholfen worden war: zunächst als Kind, später als Vater von zwei Kindern, der nach einer mehr als zehn Jahre langen Karriere in der DDR im Europa des Kalten Krieges wohl kaum noch als Wissenschafter und Hochschullehrer hätte tätig sein können.

Gescheiterte Berufungskommissionen

Im Berufungsverfahren für Friedrich Katz berichtete der Vorsitzende, Gerald Stourzh, in der Kommissionssitzung am 13.10.1983 über die Absage von Katz. Es war die erste Sitzung nach Ende der Bewerbungsfrist (15.7.1983): Prof. Katz habe anlässlich seines Besuchs in Wien im Juni und in einem Telefongespräch im September mitgeteilt, dass er nach Beratungen mit seiner Familie in Chicago verbleiben wolle. Günther Hamann, Ansprechpartner von Prof. Günther Kahle aus Köln, berichtete, dass auch Kahle keine Absicht habe erkennen lassen, sich zu bewerben. Weitere „amtswegige Nachforschungen" in dieser Sache wurden eingestellt. Im Kommissionsbericht vom 24.5.1984 an das Bundesministerium wurde die Arbeit der glücklosen Findkommission so zusammengefasst:

> „Auch hatten einzelne Mitglieder der Kommission gemäß UOG §27 (1) nach weiteren geeigneten Kandidaten im In- und Ausland nachgeforscht. Im Zuge dieser Bemühungen wurde zunächst Professor Friedrich Katz, Chicago, der bekanntlich Österreicher ist, und sodann Professor Günther Kahle, Köln, befragt, ob sie eine Berufung ernsthaft in Erwägung ziehen würden. Die Antworten beider waren negativ."[18]

Die Kommission hatte im Ausschreibungstext der Professur für „Außereuropäische Geschichte unter besonderer Berücksichtigung Lateinamerikas" vom

[17] Archiv der Universität Wien, Geisteswissenschaftliches Dekanat Zl. 52-1982/83 (Sch. 46), Berufungskommissionen 1982 bis 1984.

[18] Ebenda.

3.5.1983 wohl auf Wunsch der Professorenkurie als weiteres Erfordernis „die Bereitschaft zur Koordination und Kooperation mit bereits am Institut für Geschichte bestehenden Schwerpunkten zur außereuropäischen Geschichte (insbes. Entdeckungsgeschichte, europäische Überseegeschichte, Geschichte Nordamerikas)“ festgeschrieben.[19] Bemerkenswert ist auch, dass die Beherrschung von Spanisch und Portugiesisch gefordert wurde – eine Kombination, welche BewerberInnen aus Brasilien bevorzugte, jedoch nicht den Usancen der damaligen internationalen Amerikanistik entsprach: Französisch und Spanisch waren damals neben Englisch die viel wichtigeren Arbeitssprachen dieses Fachgebiets. Beworben haben sich in der Folge acht Herren aus Deutschland, Österreich und den Niederlanden, von denen sechs zu einem öffentlichen Anhörungsvortrag eingeladen wurden: Raymond Th. Buve, Gerhard Drekonja, Hans-Otto Kleinmann, Reinhard Liehr, Horst Pietschmann und Hans-Jürgen Puhle. Die Vorträge fanden im Jänner 1984 statt. In der konfliktreichen Kommissionssitzung am 26.01.1984 wurde ein Dreiervorschlag erstellt, dem drei Separatvoten gegenüberstanden. Die beiden Erstgereihten sagten aufgrund der mangelnden Ausstattung (eine Bibliotheksdotation von ATS 350.000 sei zu gering für eine neue Professur, das Gehalt sei ebenfalls zu gering) ab. Mit dieser halbherzigen Ausstattungsentscheidung ging das Geschick des Lateinamerika-Lehrstuhls in die Alltagsmühlen der Universität Wien über. Seit der Emeritierung von Gerhard Drekonja im Jahr 2006 ist die Stelle vakant. Eine Berufungskommission, nach zwei Ausschreibungen auch in unterschiedlicher Besetzung, in der man sich auf die Bezeichnung „Geschichte der Amerikas“ geeinigt hatte, ist inzwischen gescheitert.

Nichts oder Zukunft?

Ein Blick in die Zukunft: Das, was es überall in den USA, aber zum Beispiel auch an der ehrwürdigen Sorbonne zu Paris gibt, nämlich *chairs*, per Namen ausgewiesene Lehrstühle, die neue Fächer anlocken und alte Fächer mit großen Namen aufwerten, gibt es meines Wissens an der Universität Wien nur für Europastudien.[20] Vielleicht ist das mit Grund dafür, wieso die Bewerbungslage bei den beiden Versuchen, die ursprünglich „Lehrstuhl für Außereuropäische Geschichte unter besonderer Berücksichtigung Lateinamerikas“ genannte Stelle

---

[19] Archiv der Universität Wien, Dekanat der Geisteswissenschaftlichen Fakultät der Universität Wien ZL 52/1-82/83, Ausschreibungstext vom 3. Mai 1983.

[20] Franz Vranitzky-Chair for European Studies an der Universität Wien.

nachzubesetzen, unter anderem nicht befriedigend international war. Es wäre daher zu wünschen, dass sich die Universität Wien dazu durchringt, einen Friedrich Katz-Chair für die Geschichte Lateinamerikas einzurichten. Derart könnte Exzellenz aus Amerikanistik vielleicht auch in Wien gedeihen.

Foto/Photo: ©John Boyer, 2011
Grab Friedrich Katz' am Wiener Zentralfriedhof: Tor 2, Gruppe 15a, 3. Reihe, Nummer 42.
Friedrich Katz' tomb at Vienna's Central Cemetery: Gate 2, Group 15a, 3rd Row, Number 42.

Friedrich Katz at the University of Vienna. From Excellence to Non-Existence

Martina Kaller

What were the roles played by Vienna and its university in the life of Friedrich Katz?[1] As is well known, Katz was born in Vienna in 1927 and spent the first three years of his life here. Another biographical fact familiar to many is Katz' return with his family to Vienna in the late 1940s and his subsequent graduation from the University of Vienna. The fact that he left Vienna again in 1956 did not mean that the ties that linked him to the city and even – if to an understandably lesser degree – to the University were cut for ever. On the contrary, Katz kept returning to Vienna in the decades that followed. He and his family left many traces here, which it will be the task of future research to document in detail. In what follows I will be attempting to give an overview of the role Vienna University played in Friedrich Katz' life.

In the University Archives three files deal with Friedrich Katz: 1. his enrolment form (the "Nationale") for the years 1949–1954;[2] 2. the documentation of his doctoral viva voce;[3] and 3. the master data sheet[4] that tells us he was visiting professor at the Department of History in the summer term of 1981. In addition to this there are the minutes of a search committee (with two calls), whose task was to fill the "Chair of Non-European History, with particular attention to Latin America", the only professorship at an Austrian university for the history of Latin America. Being conversant with academic practice in the USA, Friedrich Katz, the original prime candidate for the post, which had been created in the early 1980s, was acutely aware of the importance of professorships focussed on special issues and/or regions. He knew that chairs such as this one are both an indispensable precondition for a specifically Americanistic profile to develop in research and academic tuition and a sine qua non for contributions to the discipline to gain recognition from the relevant international community.

---

[1] I would like to thank my colleague Gernot Heiß for his help in my research, without which it would have been much more difficult for me to provide answers to these questions.

[2] Archiv der Universität Wien, Inskriptionsblatt /"Nationale", Philosophical Faculty, "Nationale" Winter Term 1949/50 (ordered alphabetically).

[3] Archiv der Universität Wien, Rigorosenakt 18.955, Friedrich Katz, January 26, 1954, to December 22, 1954.

[4] Archiv der Universität Wien, Personalakt 4390, Friedrich Katz (1981) K 525.

Before I revert to the chronological sequence of events I would like to point out that I have been a witness to the saga unfolding around what might be called the "Friedrich Katz Chair" only since 1989. Everything before that year must and can be faithfully reconstructed from archive material. This means that the knowledge I have of the search committees for the visiting professorship and for the "Chair of Non-European History, with particular attention to Latin America" is based exclusively on their minutes. The latter is the only successful one to date: after a second call, the Chair was awarded to Gerhard Drekonja in 1990. Since he retired into emeritus status five years ago, I have been the sole habilitated assistant in this field. All attempts to fill the vacancy have proved unsuccessful to date, not least because of the half-heartedness shown in the handling of invitations and appointments. And so the chair, whose emphasis on Latin America makes it almost unique in German speaking countries, continues to be vacant. This is particularly regrettable now when the summer of 2012 will see the International Congress of Americanists (ICA) convened in Vienna for the third time (following on from 1908 and 1960) and at the University of Vienna itself for the very first time.

The first of the three great round tables to be held at the 54th ICA in Vienna will be devoted to Friedrich Katz. The honour of opening that session will fall to me, as the president of the 54th ICA, together with my colleagues from the Katz-Center of the University of Chicago and the Colegio de México; we will be commemorating the undisputed doyen of Mexican historiography in the very city that Katz himself considered to be the fundamental reference point of his life. At his express wish, Friedrich Katz, who passed away on Oktober 16, 2010 in Philadelphia, US, was laid to rest in Vienna's *Zentralfriedhof*.

Friedrich Katz made several attempts in the course of his life to return to Vienna. He himself believed, as he put it in a conversation, that he had twice been expelled from Austria. At the time of the first expulsion he was a very young child. This puts him in the category of the "Überleber", Ivan Illich's literal translation of "survivor". As was the case with Katz, Illich was very much someone for whom living was a deliberate act, he was no passive survivor of Austro-Fascism and Nazism. Illich incidentally never returned to Austria.[5] The second "expulsion" – Katz' term – was nurtured in the soil of Austria's "twice suppressed past", when representatives at the University of the "post-war clerical-conservative restoration with an anti-Semitic subtext"[6] botched his viva voce results.

---

[5] Kaller-Dietrich, Martina: *Ivan Illich (1927–2002). Sein Leben, sein Denken*, Bibliothek der Provinz, Weitra/Wien 2008.

[6] Stadler, Friedrich: Philosophie – Zwischen „Anschluss“ und Ausschluss, Restauration und Innovation, in: Grandner, Margarete/Heiss, Gernot/Rathkolb, Oliver (eds.): *Zukunft mit*

Studies at the University: 1949 to 1954

Friedrich Katz was lucky in that his parents, Bronia and Leo Katz, left Austria as early as 1933. His CV, which he handed in together with his doctoral thesis in 1954 to register for the viva voce, reveals that he attended elementary school in Paris, High School in New York and the Lycée Français in Mexico City, leaving in 1945. He obtained his Bachelor of Arts in New York and after another one-year course at the prestigious Escuela Nacional de Antropología e Historia (ENAH) in Mexico, Friedrich Katz enrolled at the Philosophical Faculty of Vienna University to study ethnology. He was then 22 years of age and had already a good command of the working languages indispensable to an Americanist, French, English and Spanish. He was older and certainly better equipped for his studies than the average run of his fellow students. His *Studienbuch* [Course Record Book] documents his academic progress without displaying anything unusual.

The same does not apply to his *Rigorosenakt*,[7] the documentation of his doctorate. The supervisor of his thesis, Wilhelm Koppers, awarded it top marks ("Excellent") and called it, in an assessment of February 22, 1954, "the best study of Aztec sociology currently available." He topped this by recommending the thesis for publication in book form.

Father Wilhelm Koppers (1886–1961) was a close collaborator of Father Wilhelm Schmidt (1868–1954), the founder of the Vienna *Kulturkreis* school. In his assessment of Friedrich Katz' thesis Koppers notes, with a brief genuflection before Schmidt's main area of interest: "This thesis [...] also offers interesting suggestions about old-world cultures." Koppers gave the thesis credit for interesting suggestions, not for genuine insights; Katz' sociology of the Aztecs of the 15th and 16th centuries is, after all, an analysis of economic and social conditions in the long century of Meso-America's primary colonization and has a patent historical-materialistic subtext. Anti-evolutionist speculations on monotheistic inclinations on the part of the "most primitive" cultures and on their script-less diffusion[8] (as upheld by Diffusion theory) of the sort Koppers had been initiated into by Schmidt in the ambience of the Societas Verbi Divini had no place in Katz' thesis. The Societas was a missionary order with seats in Fribourg in Switzerland, St. Augustin near Bonn and St. Gabriel in Mödling

Altlasten. Die Universität Wien 1945 bis 1955 (=Querschnitte 19), Studienverlag, Innsbruck et al. 2005, 121-136, here 131 [my translation].

[7] AUW, Rigorosenakt Katz [my translation].

[8] None of the five Mesoamerican civilizations were script-less.

near Vienna. André Gingrich, former deputy head of the Department of Social and Cultural Anthropology at the University of Vienna, has called the Vienna *Kulturkreis* school a "network with some of the trappings of a secret society" and a "doctrinaire discipline", which had become a "pillar of Austrofascism and its alliances" (Mussolini) in the late colonialist context of the politics of missionary evangelicalization.[9]

Less than two months after Koppers had completed his assessment of Katz' thesis, Robert Heine-Geldern put his signature to it, thereby validating Koppers' verdict of "Excellent". Heine-Geldern (1885–1968), who had fled Vienna in 1938, was the one figure among the Viennese Diffusionists with a pronounced international profile. Koppers had returned after the end of the war to Austria from Switzerland to resume his position as chair of the Department of Ethnology at Vienna University; Heine-Geldern, by contrast, had to wait until late 1950 before he was appointed associate professor. In 1946, while still in the USA, he had used his influence to persuade the Wenner-Gren Foundation for Anthropological Research in New York to purchase *Wartenstein* Castle near Gloggnitz as a conference venue.[10] It was 1955 before Heine-Geldern was appointed to a full professorship (a position he had actually held already long before he was expelled by the Nazis).

It is just conceivable that Katz had hoped to graduate in Vienna *sub auspiciis Praesidentis*, a particularly honorific form of PhD graduation reserved for doctoral candidates with the most outstanding academic achievements.[11] If this plan had succeeded, it would have entitled Katz to a post as university assistant. As it was, the *Philosophicum*, the second major examination subject in Katz' doctoral viva voce, which he took on December 4, 1954, scuppered this plan. The mark awarded to Katz by Leo Gabriel (1902–1987), the main examiner in this part of his viva voce and then chair of Philosophy, was no more than "Sufficient", which meant that Katz barely passed in Philosophy and

---

[9] Gingrich, Andre: Remigranten und Ehemalige: Zäsuren und Kontinuitäten in der universitären Völkerkunde Wiens nach 1945, in: Grandner, Margarete/Heiss, Gernot/Rathkolb, Oliver (eds.): *Zukunft mit Altlasten. Die Universität Wien 1945 bis 1955* (=Querschnitte 19), Studienverlag, Innsbruck et al. 2005, 260-272, here 263 [my translation].

[10] Gingrich, Remigranten, 264-266.

[11] Originally introduced in the seventeenth century as *promotio sub auspiciis Imperatoris* in Cisleithania (and as *promotio sub auspiciis Regis* in Transleithania), this graduation form had fallen into disuse with the end of the Hapsburg monarchy in 1918 and had only been revived in 1952 in the form still practised today.

Psychology, the second part of the viva voce. No minutes were kept of examinations in those days, which is why there is no room even for conjecture as to the precise events. What we do know is that Leo Gabriel, who had habilitated in 1947, upheld for decades the continuity of political Catholicism at the Department of Philosophy of the University of Vienna with his holistic philosophy and his “integral logic”. Together with Erich Heintl (1912–2000), Gabriel stood for banning the teaching of Marxism and Positivism, veritable “labyrinths of philosophy” in their eyes, in Vienna. This effectively gave the ideology of the *Ständestaat*, the corporatist state, a new lease of life and created a barrier against the return and academic reintegration at the University of Vienna of a number of philosophers who had been driven from the city.[12]

In 1954 Friedrich Katz was persona non grata at the Philosophical Faculty of Vienna’s University twice over. What motivated Katz, a member of the Communist Party at the time, to move to the German Democratic Republic is not difficult to imagine, even though there is no written evidence. He once mentioned that Anna Seghers, whom he knew from their common exile in Mexico, played a role.

After two years of surviving on quite a small salary as a journalist for Vienna’s communist newspaper *Der Abend*,[13] Friedrich Katz was given a post as assistant at the Humboldt University of Berlin in 1956. Meanwhile, the above-mentioned Robert Heine-Geldern, who had retired into emeritus status, presided over XXXIVth ICA – 34th ICA in current terminology – at Vienna’s Museum of Ethnology in 1960. The proceedings fill 854 pages, but lack any evidence that the Vienna conference in July 1960 produced any innovations in the ICA’s status as an international gathering of Americanists.[14] Friedrich Katz is named as a member together with Walter Markov from Leipzig, but his name does not

[12] Stadler, Philosophie, 134.

[13] Cf. the information on previous professional activities in: Universitätsarchiv der Humboldt-Universität zu Berlin, Personalakte K 1102, Prof. Dr. Friedrich Katz (=UA HUB Personalakt Katz), “Personalbogen” [staff questionnaire].

[14] *Akten des 34. Internationalen Amerikanistenkongresses. Wien, 18.–25. Juli 1960*, Verlag Ferdinand Berger, Horn/Wien 1962. Comas, Juan: *Cien años de Congresos Internacionales de Americanistas. Ensayo histórico-crítico y bibliográfico*, Instituto de Investigaciones Históricas/Instituto de Investigaciones Antropológicas de la UNAM, México, D.F. 1974. Comas deals in detail only with those ICAs that proved innovative with regard to international Americanist Studies; the 34th ICA does not feature in his treatment. Innovations at the 54th ICA in Vienna will include a focus on Gender Studies, for which Josefina Echavarría Álvarez will act as chair.

appear in the proceedings' list of authors (Walter Markov supervised Katz' habilitation at Berlin's Humboldt University). There are several references to Katz' participation in the 34th ICA in his Humboldt University personal file.[15] The only author from the GDR with a contribution in the proceedings is Manfred Kossok from Leipzig.[16]

Berlin and the call to Vienna

Between 1956 and 1963 Friedrich Katz was a university assistant, between 1963 and 1966 a lecturer and from 1966 to 1970 a professor (from 1969 a full professor) at Berlin's Humboldt University. Friedrich Katz' "excellent" doctoral thesis was published in 1956 in the GDR under the title *Die sozialökonomischen Verhältnisse bei den Azteken im 15. und 16. Jahrhundert* (*Socio-economic conditions among the Aztecs in the 15th and 16th centuries*) by Deutscher Verlag der Wissenschaften, Berlin. Only six years later Katz was habilitated on November 28, 1962 at Berlin's Humboldt University with his first work of transatlantic diplomatic historiography: *Deutschland, Diaz und die mexikanische Revolution: Die deutsche Politik in Mexiko 1870–1920* (*Germany, Díaz and the Mexican Revolution: German policy in Mexico 1870–1920*). After his protest against the occupation of Prague by Warsaw Pact troops in 1968 Katz continued his academic career in the Americas. He spent the winter term – overshadowed as it was by the massacre on the *Plaza de las Tres Culturas* on October 2, 1968, which entered the annals of history as the *Noche de Tlatelolco* – at the Department of Political Studies of the Universidad Nacional Autónoma de México (UNAM) and became a visiting professor at the University of Texas in

---

[15] Cf. various evaluations and letters all attesting to Katz' participation in: UA HUB Personalakt Katz.

[16] Kossok's paper was published under the title *Buenos Aires und die Genesis des Kolonialbürgertums im La Plata-Gebiet* [*Buenos Aires and the genesis of the colonial bourgeoisie in the La Plata region*]. In: *Akten des 34. Internationalen Amerikanistenkongresses. Wien, 18.–25. Juli 1960*, Verlag Ferdinand Berger, Horn/Wien 1962, 814-825. As Austria did not recognize the GDR until 1975 Katz, Kossok and Markov are not listed in the 34th ICA conference proceedings as "Delegierte von Universitäten, wissenschaftlichen Instituten und Gesellschaften" [delegates of universities, scholarly institutions and societies]. Cf. Akten 34. ICA, 12-16. On the relations obtaining between Katz, Markov and Kossok in the context of Latin American Studies in the GDR see also David Mayer's article in this volume *Der Weltenläufer: Friedrich Katz und die historiographischen Debatten seiner Zeit* [*Well-Versed in Worlds: Friedrich Katz and the historiographical debates of his time*].

Austin in 1970. In 1971 he was offered the post of Professor of Latin American History at the University of Chicago. The decision to appoint a Communist and anti-Imperialist such as Friedrich Katz so soon after the tumults of 1968 can be read as an answer to the appointment of John Womack to Harvard's equivalent chair.[17]

From Chicago Katz came to Vienna in 1981 for a spell as visiting professor of "Neuere Außereuropäische Geschichte – Lateinamerika" [Modern History of Non-European Regions – Latin America]. Katz' remit included a weekly two-hour seminar at the Department of Ethnology (then no longer part of the Philosophical Faculty but of the Faculty of Integrative Studies), which was part of the teaching assignment of Walter Dostal, formerly one of Katz' fellow students and an expert on the Near East. That this visiting professorship should be linked to the Institute of History (IfG) rather than to the Departments of Ethnology or Contemporary History was the idea of the IfG's head at the time, Gerald Stourzh, who was also behind the University's efforts to enlist Katz as a regular professor. When these efforts were on the point of coming to fruition in 1983, Friedrich Katz turned down the offered chair, citing private reasons. The unusually high increase in the endowment of his chair, a defensive move by the University of Chicago, may have been a factor that made the decision easier for him.[18]

Judging from what I remember about Friedrich Katz he was swayed less by financial considerations than by the recognition of his achievements in a country that had helped him twice at a critical juncture: once, when he was a child, and the second time when he himself had two children to provide for, at a time when, after more than ten years in the GDR, career prospects for him as a scholar and university teacher in Cold War Europe were anything but promising.

---

[17] John Womack Jr. studied in Harvard and graduated with distinction. This won the author of the most important historical work of the time on the Mexican Revolution (*Zapata and the Mexican Revolution*, 1969) a professorship for the History of Latin America at his alma mater; he was given emeritus status on November 24, 2009. Three days earlier he was awarded the "1808" medal in honour of his merits for Mexico, which he presented as a gift to the courageous trade unionists of Mexico's Electrical Utility. See: *La Jornada*, November 21, 2009, 17.

[18] Archiv der Universität Wien, Geisteswissenschaftliches Dekanat Zl. 52-1982/83 (Sch. 46), "Berufungskommissionen" [Search Committees] 1982 to 1984.

More failed search committees

When the search committee in charge of the appointment process of Friedrich Katz convened for the first time after the expiry of the deadline for applications (July 15, 1983) on October 13, 1983, Gerald Stourzh reported that the candidate had rejected the offered chair. According to Stourzh, Professor Katz told him when he was in Vienna on a visit in June and in a telephone call in September that after consulting with his family he had decided to stay in Chicago. Günther Hamann, who had been deputed to contact Professor Günther Kahle in Cologne, then reported that there were no indications Kahle was even considering to apply for the post. Other "ex officio inquiries" in this matter were stopped. In the search committee's report to the Federal Ministry of May 24, 1984, the work of this hapless committee was summed up as follows:

> "Pursuant to UOG §27 (1), individual members of the search committee had launched efforts to identify suitable candidates both in Austria and abroad. In the course of this procedure, Professor Friedrich Katz, currently in Chicago, who, as is well known, is an Austrian, was asked first whether he would seriously consider applying for the post; Professor Günther Kahle, Cologne, was next in line. The answers of both scholars were negative."[19]

In the wording of the call for the "Chair of Non-European History, with particular attention to Latin America" dating from May 3, 1983, a further requirement had been inserted, arguably at the wish of the professors' curia of the search committee that "the [prospective candidate] should be willing to coordinate and cooperate with focal points of research with regard to non-European history already established at the Institute of History (notably the history of discoveries, European overseas history, the history of North America)."[20] What is also remarkable is the addition of Portuguese as a required language – a requirement that favoured applicants from Brazil and was at odds with the standard practice in international Americanistic Studies at the time, where French and Spanish in addition to English were more important as working languages of the field. This invitation resulted in eight applications from Germany, Austria and the Netherlands, all of them from males, of whom six were invited to a public hearing: Raymond Th. Buve, Gerhard Drekonja, Hans-Otto Kleinmann, Reinhard Liehr, Horst Pietschmann and Hans-Jürgen Puhle. The hearings took place in January 1984. A conflict-laden session of the

---

[19] Ibid [my translation].

[20] Archiv der Universität Wien, Dekanat der Geisteswissenschaftlichen Fakultät der Universität Wien ZL 52/1-82/83, "Ausschreibungstext" [call] of May 3, 1983 [my translation].

search committee on January 26, 1984, resulted in a shortlist containing three names and three minority recommendations. The two frontrunners subsequently bowed out, citing the chair's insufficient endowment; they felt that the library budget of ATS 350,000 and the professorial salary were equally inadequate. With this half-hearted endowment the fate of the Chair of Latin American Studies slipped into the background of the routine operation of the University of Vienna. Since Gerhard Drekonja was given emeritus status in 2006 the chair has been vacant. A search committee, which has agreed on "History of the Americas" as the name of the chair to be filled, has yet to deliver a result after two calls.

Making do with nothing or creating a future?

A glance into the future: Chairs bearing the founder's name or commemoratively named after a great representative of the discipline are ubiquitous in the USA, at the venerable Sorbonne and elsewhere; they have the great side effect of anchoring new specialist areas in the academic context of a university or of upgrading old ones. At the University of Vienna there is, to my knowledge at least, only one such chair.[21] This is perhaps one of the reasons why international applications for the "Chair of Non-European History, with particular attention to Latin America", as it was originally called, were on two occasions few in number and slow in coming. There is always hope, and in particular there is the hope that the University of Vienna will one day muster what it takes to create a "Friedrich Katz Chair of Latin American History". This might lay the foundation for excellence in Americanist Studies to flourish in Vienna.

---

[21] Franz Vranitzky Chair for European Studies at the University of Vienna.

Biographische Fragmente.
Friedrich Katz – Erinnerungen ans mexikanische Exil

Christian Kloyber

Die folgenden Gedanken zu Friedrich Katz gehen von einer sehr persönlichen Perspektive aus, basierend auf seinen biographischen Erinnerungen, denen seiner Eltern, vor allem seiner Mutter Bronia, und von Wegbegleitern aus dem mexikanischen Exil. Diese Fragmente entstammen einer langjährigen Freundschaft aus der Ferne und einem gemeinsamen historischen Verständnis, einer Übereinkunft, die uns viele Jahre begleitete, in Mexiko und bei den wenigen Treffen in Wiener Kaffeehäusern. Während dieses Austauschs stand stets Mexiko im Mittelpunkt der Erzählung, ein uns ebenso vertrauter wie entfernter, doch immer präsenter Ort gesellschaftlicher, politischer, kultureller und historischer Dimension. In erster Linie diskutierten wir über die Mexikanische Revolution (Friedrich Katz) und über das Exil als kulturelle Identität (Christian Kloyber) und verbanden so exemplarisch und unausgesprochen die jeweils eigene Biographie mit dem uns Gemeinsamen.

„Sie werden sehen, Mexiko wird Sie nicht mehr loslassen", lautete die treffsichere Prognose, die mir Bronia Katz 1977 kurz vor meiner Abreise nach Mexiko mitgab. Ihre Zuversicht stellte auch die Weichen dafür, dass ich mich der Dokumentation des österreichischen (und deutschsprachigen europäischen) Exils in Mexiko zwischen 1938 und 1945 widmen sollte.[1] Den entscheidenden Anstoß dazu gab Bronia Katz als langjährige ehrenamtliche Mitarbeiterin des Dokumentationsarchivs des österreichischen Widerstandes (DÖW), deren eigene Biographie ebenfalls Vertreibung, Exil in Mexiko und mühevolle Rückkehr nach Österreich widerspiegelte. Diese Fragmente von politischem Widerstand, persönlichem Schicksal und Courage in einem zeitgeschichtlichen Kontext zu sehen und zu bewahren, war eine der Aufgaben, denen sie sich im DÖW widmete. Aus eigener politischer Überzeugung und der starken Motivation, das Erlebte nicht in Vergessenheit geraten zu lassen, waren ihr die mexikanischen Erfahrungen selbst drei Dekaden später immer noch höchst präsent. Das DÖW war 1963 ausschließlich auf Initiative von Widerstandskämpfern gegen den Nationalsozia-

[1] Vgl. Kloyber, Christian: Exilforschung, in: Gerhard Drekonja (Hg.): *Lateinamerikanistik. Der österreichische Weg*, LIT, Wien 2005, 65-78.

lismus, von Überlebenden und Vertriebenen gegründet worden.[2] Noch 1975, im dreißigsten Jahr nach Kriegsende, zählte es zu den wenigen Orten systematischer Dokumentation und Forschung in Österreich.

Die Kombination aus Vertreibung durch die Nationalsozialisten, dem politischen Engagement auf den Stationen vor 1940 und dem Exil in Mexiko ist ein durchgehendes Leitmotiv, das auch Bronias Sohn Friedrich, wenn auch in anderer Weise, Zeit seines Lebens bewegte. An seine Entwurzelung erinnerte Friedrich Katz seine Gesprächspartner nur selten. Seine Eltern und er waren erst 1949 aus Mexiko nach Österreich zurückgekehrt. Vor der Vertreibung aus Europa hatten sie in Berlin und Paris Station gemacht, dann in New York und ab 1940 in Mexiko. Als er mit 22 Jahren nach Österreich zurückkehrte und an der Universität Wien immatrikulierte, hatte Friedrich Katz noch nie eine deutschsprachige Schule besucht. In eine „Heimat" zurückzukehren, deren Sprache zuhause zwar immer als intime Familiensprache gesprochen wurde, die er aber nie im Unterricht erlernt oder gar vorher im Geburtsland hätte anwenden können, löste Unsicherheit, Distanzierung und Fremdheit aus, die bewältigt werden mussten:

> „Das Problem, die Dissertation in Deutsch zu schreiben, und überhaupt in ein Land zu kommen, dessen Sprache ich zwar zu Hause sprach, ohne sie jemals in einer Schule erlernt zu haben, war schwer zu bewältigen. Zudem hat doch mein Beruf durchaus mit sprachlichem Ausdruck zu tun. Es kam noch etwas hinzu. Meine Aussprache ist, wie Sie vielleicht merken werden, zwar keine ausländische, aber auch keine österreichische. Ein Deutscher würde sagen, ich bin ein Wiener, ein Wiener würde sagen, ich bin ein Deutscher. [...] Man gehört nirgendwo dazu."[3]

Friedrich Katz hatte an der Escuela Nacional de Antropología e Historia in Mexiko-Stadt zu studieren begonnen, ehe er an der Universität Wien studierte und 1954 dort promovierte.[4] Nachdem er das Studienfach Völkerkunde abgeschlossen hatte, spezialisierte er sich zunächst auf alt-mesoamerikanische und

---

[2] Bailer-Galanda, Brigitte/Neugebauer, Wolfgang: 40 Jahre Dokumentationsarchiv des österreichischen Widerstandes 1963–2003, in: Dokumentationsarchiv des österreichischen Widerstandes (Hg.): *40 Jahre Dokumentationsarchiv des österreichischen Widerstandes 1963–2003*, DÖW, Wien 2003, 26-37, hier 26.

[3] Kaiser, Konstantin: Interview mit Friedrich Katz über die Freie Jugend in Mexiko, 22. Dezember 1984 (Teilabdruck), in: Dokumentationsarchiv des österreichischen Widerstandes (Hg.): *Österreicher im Exil. Mexiko 1938–1947. Eine Dokumentation*, DÖW, Wien 2002, 239-242, hier 239.

[4] Ausführlich dazu siehe den Beitrag von Martina Kaller in diesem Band *Friedrich Katz an der Universität Wien. Von der Exzellenz ins Nichts.*

sechs Jahre später, mit seiner Habilitation aus Geschichtswissenschaften, auf mexikanische Geschichte. Die historische Rekonstruktion der Mexikanischen Revolution wurde schließlich zu seiner wissenschaftlichen Heimat, wenn ihm auch das Exilland Mexiko selbst wohl nicht die „Heimat" als solche ersetzte.

Es fiel ihm nicht leicht, sich als Jugendlicher im *wohltemperierten* mexikanischen Exil wohlzufühlen. Die Jahre vor 1940 waren noch mit dem Gefühl einer unbeschwerten Freiheit verbunden gewesen, die er als Kind und Schüler mit französischen oder New Yorker Gleichaltrigen und Erwachsenen erleben konnte. Das Leben während der Kriegsjahre in Mexiko empfand er hingegen als eine Art Ghetto. Er besuchte keine mexikanische Schule mit mexikanischen Mitschülern, sondern die französische. Umgeben von seinen Eltern und den ebenso vertriebenen exilierten Freunden und Bekannten blieb er möglichen mexikanischen Spielgefährten und Freunden fremd und entfernt. Er selbst bezeichnete das als „Emigrationsghetto". Dieses Gefühl der Ausgeschlossenheit sollte sich erst später legen, als sich für ihn berufliche Karriere und Forschungsinteresse abzeichneten und damit auch die Integration in das universitäre Leben in Mexiko gelang: „Erst als ich nach meiner Matura in den USA ein Jahr studiert hatte und (danach) in eine mexikanische Hochschule ging, begann ich mich völlig zu integrieren. Aber vorher war es sehr schwierig."[5]

„Man gehört nirgendwo dazu..."

Während Politik und Wissenschaft in Mexiko schon viel früher und mehrfach ihre Anerkennung und Bewunderung für einen *extranjero*, einen Ausländer, der sich sein Leben lang mit ihrer Geschichte auseinandersetzte, öffentlich bezeugt hatte, unternahm das offizielle Österreich nichts zur Ehrung des Vertriebenen.[6] Anstelle einer einige Jahre zuvor vom österreichischen Exilforscher Konstantin Kaiser angeregten und von der zuständigen Behörde abgelehnten Auszeichnung[7] erhielt Friedrich Katz, wie jeder andere Absolvent der Universität Wien, 50 Jahre nach seiner Promovierung im Jahr 2004 das Goldene Doktordiplom seiner

---

[5] Kaiser, Interview mit Friedrich Katz, 239.

[6] Kaller, Martina: Österreichs und Mexikos diplomatische Verflechtungen, in: María y Campos, Alfonso de/Rivero Weber, Lilia/Feest, Christian (Hg.): *Der altmexikanische Federkopfschmuck*, ZKF, Altenstadt 2012, 1-4.

[7] Kaiser, Konstantin: *Zwischen Heimweh und neuer Erkenntnis – Österreichische Exilliteratur in Lateinamerika*, Salzburg 2002, in: https://www.sbg.ac.at/exil/l5012.pdf, 2 (Zugriff 5. April 2012).

Alma Mater. Sein berechtigtes Urteil, dass die Universität Wien auch für ihn als Historiker nicht besonders interessant war, mag immer noch zutreffen:

> „Für die moderne Geschichte Lateinamerikas hatten die Wiener Bibliotheken nicht viel zu bieten. Ich habe oft das Gefühl gehabt, dass mit dem Tod Maximilians Lateinamerika für österreichische Bibliothekare unterging. Für das Studium der altamerikanischen Kulturen allerdings erwiesen sich die Wiener Nationalbibliothek und die Wiener Universität als Fundgrube, [...] was mir erlaubte, meine Dissertation über die sozioökonomischen Verhältnisse bei den Azteken im 15. und 16. Jahrhundert fertig zu stellen.“[8]

Es passt ins Bild, dass Friedrich Katz 1988 die höchste Auszeichnung verliehen wurde, die Mexiko an Ausländer vergibt: den *Águila Azteca*-Orden. Kein besserer Zeitpunkt hätte gewählt werden können. 50 Jahre nach dem „Anschluss“ Österreichs an Nazideutschland gedachte das offizielle Mexiko des Schicksals der Vertriebenen und erinnerte auch an den offiziellen Protest, den Mexiko unter Präsident General Lázaro Cárdenas durch einen seiner ausgezeichneten Diplomaten, Isidro Fabela, vor dem Völkerbund eingebracht hatte. Es war auch Friedrich Katz, der 1976 in der *Zeitschrift für Lateinamerika Wien* als Erster über Quellen und zeitgeschichtliche Voraussetzungen des mexikanischen Protests gegen das Verschwinden Österreichs von der Landkarte des Völkerbunds publizierte.[9] An das Schicksal der Mexiko-Exilanten und an die Protagonisten der mexikanischen Außenpolitik zwischen 1938 und 1945 erinnern heute im 22. Wiener Gemeindebezirk die Gilberto-Bosques-Promenade und die Isidro-Fabela-Promenade. Friedrich Katz hatte auf die besondere Rolle beider Diplomaten mehrmals hingewiesen. Unterstützung für diese Verkehrsflächenbenennung kam später insbesondere vom DÖW.[10]

Geehrt hat „ihren“ Wissenschaftler letztlich nur die Stadt Wien, indem sie im Herbst 2011 ein ehrenvolles Festsymposion veranstaltete. Auf Initiative der mexikanischen Botschaft in Österreich veranstaltete sie in Zusammenarbeit mit den Lateinamerikanisten der Historisch-Kulturwissenschaftlichen Fakultät der

---

[8] Katz, Friedrich: Lateinamerikanistik-Studium in Wien in den 1950ern, in: Gerhard Drekonja (Hg.): *Lateinamerikanistik. Der österreichische Weg*, LIT, Wien 2005, 21-24, hier 22-23.

[9] Katz, Friedrich: Mexiko und der Anschluss Österreichs, in: *Zeitschrift für Lateinamerika Wien* 11 (1976), 113-120.

[10] Beide Straßenbenennungen (2003 und 2005) gehen auf die Initiative von Christian Kloyber zurück. Der Antrag auf die Verkehrsflächenbenennungen wurde vom Dokumentationsarchiv des Österreichischen Widerstandes und der damaligen mexikanischen Botschafterin in Österreich und späteren Außenministerin Mexikos, Patricia Espinosa Cantellano, unterstützt.

Universität Wien am 20. Oktober 2011 ein Gedenksymposium im Alten Rathaus.[11] Nur wenigen der Mitwirkenden war bewusst, dass im gleichen Gebäude Friedrich Katz' Mutter an der Aufarbeitung der Geschichte des österreichischen Widerstands und des Exil mitgearbeitet hatte, befindet sich doch das Dokumentationsarchiv des österreichischen Widerstandes nur wenige Schritte vom Festsaal im Alten Rathaus entfernt.

„Man gehört nirgendwo dazu…", lautete die Erkenntnis vieler Rückkehrer am Ende des Zweiten Weltkriegs, die sich nach den Rissen und Brüchen in ihren Biographien der Frage stellen mussten, wohin ihre Exilerfahrung sie führen würde. Als die Familie Katz das mexikanische Exil 1949 verließ, war die Mehrheit der österreichischen Emigranten – unter ihnen der befreundete Journalist Bruno Frei[12] – schon ab 1946, oft auf gefährlichen Umwegen, nach Wien zurückgekehrt. Die schwere Herzerkrankung von Friedrichs Vater Leo Katz verzögerte jedoch die geplante Ausreise nach Israel, wo man im eben gegründeten jüdischen Staat einen Neubeginn versuchen wollte. Während Gepäck und Überseekoffer direkt nach Israel verschifft wurden, rafften sich Leo, Bronia und Friedrich Katz auf, vorher noch einmal nach Wien zu reisen:

> „Als wir dann endlich so weit waren […] sind wir mit dem Schiff von Mexiko nach Kuba gefahren. Dort waren wir zwei Wochen, wir mussten auf ein polnisches Kreuzfahrtschiff warten. Als wir nach Österreich gekommen sind, wollten wir doch, bevor man sich nach Israel einschiffte, mit all den Freunden wieder Kontakt aufnehmen. In Wien hat man zu Leo gesagt: ‚Wir brauchen dich, und du solltest unbedingt dableiben. Und es ist lächerlich, klimatisch ist Österreich viel günstiger als Israel.' Und so haben wir beschlossen, doch in Österreich zu bleiben. Wir besaßen aber noch die Schiffskarten für Israel – alle unsere Sachen waren außerdem dort angekommen. […] Tatsache ist, dass wir in Israel sehr wenig gesehen haben, denn mein Mann hat diese Wochen die meiste Zeit als Kranker im Bett verbracht. Er hat das Klima wirklich nicht vertragen. Und dann war er auch sehr enttäuscht über die Möglichkeit dort zu arbeiten. Er hatte sich innerlich schon damit abgefunden, im ‚nazistischen' Österreich zu bleiben."[13]

[11] Die Beiträge von Javier Garciadiego, David Mayer und Berthold Molden im vorliegenden Band gehen auf ihre Vorträge im Rahmen dieser Veranstaltung zurück.

[12] Frei, Bruno: *Der Papiersäbel. Autobiographie*, Fischer, Frankfurt a. Main 1972.

[13] Kaiser, Konstantin: Interview mit Bronia Katz, 15. November 1984 (Teilabdruck), in: Dokumentationsarchiv des österreichischen Widerstandes (Hg.): *Österreicher im Exil. Mexiko 1938–1947. Eine Dokumentation*, DÖW, Wien 2002, 576-577, hier 577.

Freie Jugend im mexikanischen Exil

Von Beginn an war Friedrich Katz Mitglied der Freien Jugend Mexiko; ein politisches, ein kulturelles und auch ein sprachliches Zuhause war damit vorhanden. Die brennenden Fragen, die in der Jugendgruppe besprochen wurden, waren Katz zufolge nicht in erster Linie politischer Natur. Vielmehr suchte man nach Orientierung für die Zukunft: „Sollten wir uns als Deutsche oder Österreicher fühlen oder waren wir jüdische Emigranten, die nun Mexikaner waren? Und wenn wir keine Mexikaner waren, so waren wir heimatlose Juden, aber auf keinen Fall Deutsche oder Österreicher.“[14] Diese Fragen und Zweifel beruhten nicht nur auf einer möglichen, aber unbegründeten existenziellen Angst im Exilland, sie hatten immer auch politische und historische Grundlagen. Es war bezeichnend, dass man sich „Freie Jugend Mexiko“ nannte und die Bezeichnung einer nationalen Zugehörigkeit vermied. Weder deutsch noch österreichisch wollte die Freie Jugend Mexikos sein.

Friedrichs Vater, Leo Katz, hatte durch seine langjährige Mitgliedschaft bei der Kommunistischen Partei Deutschlands viel engere Kontakte zur deutschen Gruppe in Mexiko (Bewegung Freies Deutschland [Alemania Libre]) als zu den österreichischen Exilanten, die sich in der Acción Republicana Austriaca de México zusammengeschlossen hatten. Er blickte mit Pessimismus auf die Frage, welche Rolle der antifaschistische Widerstand in Deutschland und in Österreich spielen würde. Könnten nach dem Krieg demokratische deutsche und österreichische Gesellschaften mit einer antifaschistischen und antirassistischen Grundhaltung aufgebaut werden? Dieser Pessimismus war einer der Gründe, die Leo Katz nicht an eine Rückkehr nach Österreich denken ließen. Ganz im Gegensatz zu seinem Vater setzte Friedrich Katz in den Jahren des mexikanischen Exils auf den Widerstand gegen Hitler. Die österreichischen Exilanten in London berichteten ja in ihren Sendungen und Publikationen von Sabotageaktionen und dem Widerstandskampf in der „Heimat“.

Dieser Optimismus erwies sich für Friedrich Katz jedoch als trügerisch, als er tatsächlich nach Österreich zurückkehrte und damit jenes Ziel seiner mexikanischen Jahre verwirklichte, das zur oben zitierten Scheu vor österreichischer Identität in gewissem Widerspruch zu stehen scheint:

> „Wir hatten ja eine Jugendgruppe, in der Deutsche und Österreicher zusammen waren, und die Österreicher waren eigentlich nicht losgetrennt. Wir waren zwei Österreicher in dieser Gruppe und wir haben uns beide, zumindest ab 1943, schon als

---

[14] Kaiser, Interview mit Friedrich Katz, 242.

Österreicher gefühlt, nicht als Deutsche. Mein Ziel war es, irgendwann nach Wien zurückzukehren, das ich gar nicht kannte. Ich las also alles mit Interesse, was [man] vom Roten Wien erzählte, vom Februar 1934, von Floridsdorf, vom Karl-Marx-Hof. Das wuchs in meinem Kopf zu etwas Lebhaftem an, was mir ja aus aktueller Anschauung völlig unbekannt war.“[15]

Die Geschichte tritt in der Erinnerung vor die Realpolitik. Oft betonte Friedrich Katz, dass es sich bei den Exilorganisationen in Mexiko mehr um kulturelle und soziale Gruppen handelte als um politische. Dies war wohl nicht nur im Sprachgebrauch gegenüber den mexikanischen Behörden wichtig; das Besondere am mexikanischen Exil waren ja die in der Hauptstadt geballt versammelten intellektuellen und künstlerischen Kräfte. Friedrich Katz kam mit einigen der bedeutenden Vertreter der deutschsprachigen Kultur in Kontakt: Bodo Uhse hielt literaturwissenschaftliche Vorträge, Anna Seghers las aus ihren Texten, Bruno Frei referierte über europäische Geschichte und Kultur. Theateraufführungen und Konzerte zeitgenössischer Musik von Arnold Schönberg, Marcel Rubin und Ruth Schönthal waren regelmäßiger Bestandteil des Exillebens.

1945 erschien im deutschsprachigen Exilverlag El Libro Libre die letzte große Publikation Egon Erwin Kischs: seine *Entdeckungen in Mexiko*. Der „rasende Reporter“, Schriftsteller, Zauberer und literarische Unterhaltungskünstler war auch im mexikanischen Exil eine viel bewunderte und oft ebenso umstrittene charismatische Figur. Der Prager Altösterreicher, Kommunist und jüdische Kosmopolit erwies mit seinen Reportagen aus Mexiko dem Gast- und Exilland Referenz und Dankbarkeit – nicht in der sozialkritischen Schärfe eines B. Traven, nicht mit der Sentimentalität eines Malcolm Lowry (*Unter dem Vulkan*) oder des enttäuschten Gustav Regler (*Vulkanisches Land*), noch mit der Radikalität eines Antonin Artaud (*Reise ins Land der Tarahumaras*). Die journalistische Kunst des „rasenden Reporters“ bestand vielmehr in seinem tiefen Einfühlungsvermögen, akribischer Recherche und einer fesselnden, erzählenden Sprache.

Damit hatte Egon Erwin Kisch eine Vorgabe geschaffen, der noch ein wissenschaftlich fundiertes und zeitgeschichtliches Werk über Mexiko an die Seite zu stellen war. Mag sein, dass Friedrich Katz auch diese Anregung irgendwie aufgriff, ist doch in seinen Texten eine große narrative Neigung erkennbar genauso wie das Lesevergnügen während der Quellenarbeit. Jedenfalls ist auch das einzige Mal, dass Friedrich Katz in Mexiko auf einer Bühne stand, zumindest indirekt Egon Erwin Kisch zuzuschreiben. Als nämlich 1945 der 60. Geburtstag

[15] Kaiser, Interview mit Friedrich Katz, 240.

Kischs in Mexiko mit einer theatralischen Überraschungsaufführung begangen wurde, stand der junge Friedrich Katz als Komparse auf der Bühne. Zur Aufführung im Heinrich Heine Club kam Kischs von Bodo Uhse dramatisierte Aufdeckungsreportage *Der Fall des Generalstabschefs Redl.*[16] Diese Erfahrungen mögen dazu beigetragen haben, dass Katz in späteren Jahren zur Überzeugung kam, er habe selbst keine politische Position eingenommen, sondern eben eine soziale und kulturelle.

Mexiko im Herzen

Es war wohl ein bestimmtes Ereignis mit ausschlaggebend dafür, dass die Geschichte der Mexikanischen Revolution und der mexikanischen Diplomatie für Friedrich Katz zum Lebensinhalt wurde. Als die Rückkehr nach Europa weder in Österreich noch in der Deutschen Demokratischen Republik so verlief, wie er es gehofft hatte, mochte dieser besondere Moment im mexikanischen Exil eine wichtige Rolle gespielt haben. Friedrich Katz erinnerte sich lebhaft daran:

> „Als Deutschland ganz Frankreich besetzte, wurden Gilberto Bosques und sämtliche Konsulatsangestellte über zwei Jahre lang im deutschen Bad Godesberg interniert, wo sie in völliger Isolation lebten. Als sie 1944 endlich gegen deutsche Agenten ausgetauscht wurden und nach Mexiko zurückkehren konnten, versammelten sich Tausende Flüchtlinge zu ihrer Begrüßung. Ich erinnere mich daran, dass meine Eltern mit mir in der Nacht, als Bosques ankam, zum Bahnhof Buenavista in Mexiko fuhren. Tausende warteten dort viele Stunden auf die Ankunft Bosques, bis endlich der verspätete Zug angesagt wurde. Als Bosques ankam, bereiteten diejenigen, die ihm ihr Leben zu verdanken hatten, [ihm] einen triumphalen Empfang.“[17]

Gilberto Bosques stand wegen seiner humanistischen Gesinnung und politischen Überzeugung als einer der Protagonisten der Mexikanischen Revolution im diplomatischen Dienst. Im besetzten Frankreich unterstützte er als mexikanischer Konsul den antifaschistischen Widerstand, rettete tausende flüchtende Kämpfer und Kämpferinnen des Spanischen Bürgerkriegs, und trat für die Vertriebenen und Verfolgten ein. Seine politische Überzeugung folgte keinem parteipolitischen Kalkül, sondern rührte von den Prinzipien der Mexikanischen Revolution her, und sie berührte wohl auch Friedrich Katz. Die beiden verband später eine

---

[16] Egon Erwin Kisch, *Der Fall des Generalstabschefs Redl. Außenseiter der Gesellschaft. Die Verbrechen der Gegenwart*, Verlag Die Schmiede, Berlin 1924.

[17] Katz, Friedrich: Unserer Familie hat die mexikanische Politik das Leben gerettet, in: Dokumentationsarchiv des österreichischen Widerstandes (Hg.): *Österreicher im Exil. Mexiko 1938–1947. Eine Dokumentation*, DÖW, Wien 2002, 9-12, hier 11.

lebenslange Freundschaft und tiefe Wertschätzung füreinander. Ist es dieser Freundschaft zu verdanken, dass sich in späteren Jahren das Bild vom „Emigranten-Ghetto" der ersten Exiljahre veränderte? Im Vorwort zur Publikation *Exilio y cultura. El exilio cultural austriaco en México* fasste Katz seine Verbundenheit mit Mexiko folgendermaßen zusammen:

> „Für mich persönlich haben meine Jugend in Mexiko und die Herzlichkeit, mit der wir von der mexikanischen Bevölkerung aufgenommen wurden, mein Leben in vielerlei Hinsicht entscheidend geprägt. Auch als ich nach Österreich zurückkehrte, habe ich Mexiko im Geist niemals verlassen, denn meine gesamte Forschungstätigkeit, meine wissenschaftliche Arbeit, hatten in der einen oder anderen Form immer mit Mexiko zu tun."[18]

So bestätigt sich in der Lebensgeschichte von Friedrich Katz ein Zitat der aus Wien vertriebenen jüdischen Exilantin Ruth Deutsch Lechuga, die in Mexiko ihre wirkliche Heimat fand. Die Ärztin, Fotografin und Ethnologin resümierte ihre Exilerfahrung in Worten, in denen Friedrich Katz mit gemeint zu sein scheint: „In Mexiko behandelte man uns nicht wie Menschen zweiter Klasse. Wir konnten uns frei und nach unseren Möglichkeiten entfalten."[19]

---

[18] Katz, Friedich: Prólogo, in: Kloyber, Christian (Hg.): *Exilio y cultura. El exilio cultural austriaco en México*, SRE, México, D.F. 2002, 15-18, hier 18 [Übersetzung C. K].

[19] Gespräch mit Christian Kloyber, Mexiko 2006.

Friedrich Katz – Memories of the Mexican Exile

Christian Kloyber

The following thoughts about Friedrich Katz draw on deeply personal sources – Katz' own memories, those of his parents (especially his mother, Bronia) and those of his companions during his exile in Mexico. My access to these memories is owed to a friendship cultivated from afar and over many years and to a shared outlook on history, a rapport that flourished both in Mexico and during our occasional meetings in Viennese cafés. Throughout this exchange, the main issue was always Mexico, a social, political, cultural and historical cauldron that was both familiar and distant, but above all always in the very forefront of both our minds. Our main talking points were the Mexican Revolution and exile as a source of cultural identity, thus entwining each other's life story with our common interests in our discussion of concrete examples.

"You will see, Mexico will never let you go", was the unerring prognosis given to me by Bronia Katz in 1977, shortly before my first visit. This conviction of hers was also what set me up for my documentation of Austrian (and German-speaking European) exiles in Mexico between 1938 and 1945.[1] So the decisive impulse for this study came directly from Bronia Katz, the long-time associate of the Documentation Centre of Austrian Resistance (Dokumentationsarchiv des österreichischen Widerstandes, DÖW), whose own life mirrored the general history of expulsion, exile in Mexico and return to Austria. To see and preserve these fragments of political resistance, personal fate and courage in their context of contemporary history was one of the tasks she took on at the DÖW. Because of her own political conviction and the strong motivation not to let what she and others had lived through fall into oblivion, her Mexican experiences were still fresh in her mind even after thirty years. The DÖW itself had been founded in 1963 exclusively on the initiative of resistance fighters against National Socialism, of survivors and of Austrian exiles.[2] In 1975, thirty years

[1] Cf. Kloyber, Christian: Exilforschung, in: Gerhard Drekonja (ed.): *Lateinamerikanistik. Der österreichische Weg*, LIT, Wien 2005, 65-78.

[2] Bailer-Galanda, Brigitte/Neugebauer, Wolfgang: 40 Jahre Dokumentationsarchiv des österreichischen Widerstandes 1963–2003, in: Dokumentationsarchiv des österreichischen Widerstandes (ed.): *40 Jahre Dokumentationsarchiv des österreichischen Widerstandes 1963–2003*, DÖW, Wien 2003, 26-37, hier 26.

after the war, it was still one of the few places in Austria dedicated to the systematic research and documentation of this topic.

Expulsion from Austria at the hands of the Nazis, his family's political activism before 1940 and his exile in Mexico coalesced into a sort of leitmotif for Friedrich Katz that was to keep him company all his life. He rarely referred in conversation to the constant uprooting he had undergone. Before the family fled Europe they had stopped over in Berlin and Paris and after a brief sojourn in New York they had moved to Mexico in 1940. When he returned to Austria at the age of 22 and matriculated at the University of Vienna, Friedrich Katz had never been to a German-speaking school. He came "home" to a language that had always served the family for internal communication but had never been taught to him in class – a language, moreover, that he had never had the chance to use in the country of his birth. He had to come to terms with the resulting insecurity, alienation and strangeness:

> "The problems I faced writing my dissertation in German and, in general, in coming to a country whose language, although I spoke it at home, I had never learned at school were hard to cope with. They were exacerbated by the fact that my profession has so much to do with language and expression. And there was something else: as you may notice, my accent is not foreign, but it isn't Austrian either. A German would say that I was Viennese, a Viennese would say that I was German. […] You don't belong anywhere."[3]

Friedrich Katz began his studies at the Escuela Nacional de Antropología e Historia in Mexico City before going on to the University of Vienna, where he received his doctorate in 1954.[4] Having exhausted what the ethnology curriculum had to offer, he turned to ancient Mesoamerican history and, with his habilitation in Historical Sciences six years later, to Mexican history. The historical reconstruction of the Mexican Revolution eventually became his preferred academic stamping ground, even though he was never quite able to call the Mexico of his exile home.

---

[3] Kaiser, Konstantin: Interview mit Friedrich Katz über die Freie Jugend in Mexiko, December 22, 1984 (partial reproduction), in: Dokumentationsarchiv des österreichischen Widerstandes (ed.): *Österreicher im Exil. Mexiko 1938–1947. Eine Dokumentation*, DÖW, Wien 2002, 239-242, here 239 [my translation].

[4] Cf. Martina Kaller's article in this volume *Friedrich Katz an der Universität Wien. Von der Exzellenz ins Nichts* [*Friedrich Katz at the University of Vienna. From Excellence to Non-Existence*].

Mexico was, on the face of it, a *well-tempered* exile, to use his own phrase, but it was not an easy or comfortable place for the adolescent Katz. The years before 1940 had been marked by a feeling of light-hearted freedom shared alike by his French or New Yorker peers and the adults in his circle. In stark contrast, he felt he had spent the war years in Mexico in some sort of gilded cage. Instead of attending a Mexican school with Mexican classmates he went to a French school. Surrounded at home by his parents and their likewise exiled friends and acquaintances, he had next to no contact with young Mexicans and so had little chance to make Mexican friends. He referred to this situation as an "emigration ghetto". This feeling of exclusion would only lessen when his professional career and his research interests evolved and he managed to establish himself in Mexico's academia: "Only after studying in the USA for a year after my high school graduation and then attending a Mexican university did I start to become properly integrated. Before that it was very difficult."[5]

"You don't belong anywhere..."

While the political and academic elite in Mexico had repeatedly and early on expressed their appreciation and admiration for this *extranjero*, this foreigner, who spent his life studying the country's history, Austrian officialdom did nothing to honour the exiled intellectual.[6] Austrian exile-scholar Konstantin Kaiser did press for some official recognition of Katz' eminence in his field, only to be turned down by the authorities.[7] In the event, the only honour granted to Katz in the country of his birth was the Golden Doctorate Diploma (bestowed in 2004), an award open to any and all alumni of the University of Vienna on the 50th anniversary of their graduation. His perspicacious comment that the University of Vienna had its limitations for a Latin-Americanist focused on modern history may still be true today:

> "For a student of the modern history of Latin America, Vienna's libraries did not have much to offer. I often felt that, in the eyes of Austrian librarians, Latin America had gone under with Maximilian's death. For the study of the ancient American cul-

---

[5] Kaiser, Interview mit Friedrich Katz, 239 [my translation].

[6] Kaller, Martina: Österreichs und Mexikos diplomatische Verflechtungen, in: María y Campos, Alfonso de/Rivero Weber, Lilia/Feest, Christian (eds.): *Der altmexikanische Federkopfschmuck*, ZKF, Altenstadt 2012, 1-4.

[7] Kaiser, Konstantin: *Zwischen Heimweh und neuer Erkenntnis – Österreichische Exilliteratur in Lateinamerika*, Salzburg 2002, in: https://www.sbg.ac.at/exil/l5012.pdf, 2 (retrieved on April 5, 2012).

> tures, however, the National Library in Vienna and the University of Vienna turned out to be real treasure houses, […] of great help to me in finishing my dissertation about the socio-economic conditions of the Aztecs in the 15th and 16th centuries."[8]

This difference in treatment was emphasised in 1988 when Friedrich Katz received the highest distinction that Mexico awards to foreigners: the Order of the *Águila Azteca*. The moment could not have been better. 50 years after Austria's "Anschluss" with Nazi-Germany, the Mexican government commemorated the fate of the Austrians who were driven into exile and Mexico's official protest presented before the League of Nations by President Lázaro Cárdenas' diplomat Isidro Fabela. Friedrich Katz had been the first to go into print with the sources and historical conditions of this Mexican remonstration against Austria's annexation, in his article in the *Zeitschrift für Lateinamerika Wien*.[9] In today's Vienna, the *Gilberto-Bosques-Promenade* and the *Isidro-Fabela-Promenade* remind us of the fate of the exiled who found asylum in Mexico and the protagonists of Mexican foreign policy between 1938 and 1945. Friedrich Katz had repeatedly pointed out the importance of these two diplomats. The actual renaming of the public streets was eventually initiated by the DÖW.[10]

Ultimately, it was the City of Vienna that took up an initiative of the Mexican embassy and, together with the Latin-Americanists of the Faculty of Historical and Cultural Studies at the University of Vienna, organized a commemorative event at the Old Town Hall on October 20, 2011.[11] Hardly any of the organizers were aware of the fact that Friedrich Katz' mother had contributed to the documentation of the history of the Austrian resistance at this very place: the DÖW can be found only a few steps away from the *Festsaal* at the Old Town Hall.

"You don't belong anywhere…" was the conclusion of many returnees after the end of World War II. Not only did they have to face the many breaks and fault lines in their own lives, but also the question of where this experience of

---

[8] Katz, Friedrich: Lateinamerikanistikstudium in Wien in den 1950ern, in: Gerhard Drekonja (ed.): *Lateinamerikanistik. Der österreichische Weg*, LIT, Wien 2005, 21-24, here 22-23 [my translation].

[9] Katz, Friedrich: Mexiko und der Anschluss Österreichs, in: *Zeitschrift für Lateinamerika Wien* 11 (1976), 113-120.

[10] The renaming of both streets (2003 and 2005) was initiated by Christian Kloyber. The petition was supported by the DÖW and Patricia Espinosa Cantellano, then the Mexican ambassador in Austria and later foreign minister of Mexico.

[11] The contributions to this volume by Javier Garciadiego, David Mayer and Berthold Molden are based on their talks during this event.

exile would finally lead them. When the Katz family left Mexico in 1949, the majority of Austrian exiles – among them their friend, the journalist Bruno Frei[12] – had already returned to Vienna in the years following 1946, some of them by quite dangerous paths. However, the serious heart condition afflicting Friedrich's father Leo Katz delayed the family's planned departure to Israel, where they intended to make a fresh start in the recently founded Jewish state. While their luggage had been shipped directly to Israel, Leo, Bronia and Friedrich Katz decided to pay one more visit to Vienna:

> "When we had finally sorted ourselves out […], we took the ship from Mexico to Cuba. There we stayed for two weeks, waiting for a Polish cruise ship. Upon our arrival in Austria and before boarding the ship for Israel, we wanted to contact our old friends again. In Vienna they told Leo: 'We need you, and you should by all means stay here. And it's ridiculous you leaving anyway – the Austrian climate is much better than Israel's.' And so it was that we decided to stay in Austria after all. But we still had the tickets for Israel – besides, all our stuff was there. […] In fact, we saw very little of Israel, because my husband spent most of the time sick in bed. He really could not stand the climate. And he was highly disappointed with the job opportunities there. Inside, he had already come to terms with the idea of staying in 'Nazi'-Austria."[13]

"Freie Jugend Mexiko"

After his arrival as an exile in Mexico, Friedrich Katz had joined the youth organization Freie Jugend Mexiko (Free Youth Mexiko), which offered him a cultural and linguistic home. According to Katz, the burning issues that were discussed in the youth group were not primarily of a political nature. Much rather, they discussed their own future orientation: "Should we see ourselves as Germans or Austrians or were we Jewish emigrants who had now become Mexicans? And if we weren't Mexicans, were we not homeless Jews, so that the last thing we should call ourselves is Germans or Austrians?"[14] These questions and doubts were not simply the result of a natural, though unfounded, existential fear arising from their exile, but had a political and historical basis. It was signif-

---

[12] Frei, Bruno: *Der Papiersäbel. Autobiographie*, Fischer, Frankfurt a. Main 1972.

[13] Kaiser, Konstantin: Interview mit Bronia Katz, November 15, 1984 (partial reproduction), in: Dokumentationsarchiv des österreichischen Widerstandes (ed.): *Österreicher im Exil. Mexiko 1938–1947. Eine Dokumentation*, DÖW, Wien 2002, 576-577, here 577 [my translation].

[14] Kaiser, Interview mit Friedrich Katz, 242 [my translation].

icant that the group called itself "Freie Jugend Mexiko" and avoided any national reference in their denomination; they had no wish to be German or Austrian.

Because of his long membership of the Communist Party of Germany, Friedrich's father Leo Katz had much closer contacts with the Germans in Mexico (Bewegung Freies Deutschland [Alemania Libre]) than with the Austrian emigrants who had organized the Acción Republicana Austriaca de México. He was pessimistic about the possible role of the antifascist resistance in Germany and Austria. Would it be possible to build democratic German and Austrian post-war societies based on an antifascist and antiracist stance? This pessimism was one of the reasons why Leo Katz was against a return to Austria. In contrast to his father, Friedrich Katz believed in the resistance against Hitler, at least during his Mexican exile. After all, Austrian exiles in London were constantly broadcasting and publishing about acts of sabotage and resistance at "home".

Much as Friedrich Katz had cherished the idea of a return to Austria, he found that his optimism had deceived him when he did indeed return:

> "We had a youth group, in which Germans and Austrians got together, and the Austrians were not really separated. There were two of us Austrians in this group and we both felt ourselves to be Austrians, not Germans, especially after 1943. It was my goal to return to Vienna some day, although I had no knowledge of the city at all. Because of this I was interested in reading anything associated with Red Vienna, with February 1934, with [the Viennese district of] Floridsdorf or the *Karl-Marx-Hof*.[15] In my mind, these tales grew into a living picture of something I had never myself laid eyes on."[16]

In his memory, history came before realpolitik. Friedrich Katz often emphasized that the exile organizations in Mexico were cultural and social groups rather than political ones. This may not only have been a careful choice of words designed to placate the Mexican authorities, but may also indicate that the peculiarity of the Mexican exile resided precisely in those intellectual and artistic circles that congregated in the capital. Friedrich Katz came to know some of the most important representatives of German-language culture: Bodo Uhse gave

---

[15] *Das Rote Wien*, Red Vienna, refers to the mostly absolute rule of the Socialdemocratic Workers' Party (Sozialdemokratische Arbeiterpartei, SDAP) in the Austrian capital between the founding of the Republic in 1918 and February 1934, when the austrofascist regime illegalized the SDAP after a short civil war. This period is particularly known for its large investments, despite the economic crisis, in public housing and social infrastructure which it financed by special redistribution taxes. One central site of the February uprising was the municipal residential estate *Karl-Marx-Hof*.

[16] Kaiser, Interview mit Friedrich Katz, 240 [my translation].

lectures on literature, Anna Seghers read from her texts, Bruno Frei spoke on European history and culture. Theatre performances and concerts of contemporary music by Arnold Schönberg, Marcel Rubin and Ruth Schönthal were part of the exiles' everyday life.

In 1945 El Libro Libre, publishing house of the German-language exiles, brought out Egon Erwin Kisch's last great text, his *Entdeckungen in Mexiko* (*Discoveries in Mexico*). The "raging Reporter", author, magician and literary entertainer, continued to be a much-admired, controversial and charismatic figure among the Mexican exiles. The k.&k.-Austrian from Prague, Communist and Jewish cosmopolite showed his gratitude to Mexico with his journalistic reporting, which eschewed the sociocritical severity of B. Traven, the sentimentality of Malcolm Lowry (*Under the Volcano*) or of the disappointed Gustav Regler (*Vulkanisches Land*), and the radical gestures of Antonin Artaud (*Voyage to the Land of the Tarahumara*). Kisch's journalistic mastery lay in his strong empathy, his meticulous research and his captivating narrative language.

Thus Egon Erwin Kisch had set a standard which had yet to be met by a well-grounded work on Mexico's contemporary history. Perhaps Friedrich Katz seized this suggestion in some way, given the strong narrative disposition which is evident in his texts and which demonstrates his own pleasure in tackling sources. At any rate, the only time that Friedrich Katz performed on a Mexican stage can reasonably be laid at the door of Egon Erwin Kisch. During the festivities on the occasion of Kisch's sixtieth birthday a surprise performance of *Der Fall des Generalstabschefs Redl* (*The Case of the Chief of Staff Redl*), dramatized by Bodo Uhse and enacted at the Heinrich Heine Club, featured Friedrich Katz as an extra.[17] These experiences may have contributed to Katz' later opinion that he had not taken a political stance in Mexico, but a cultural and social one.

Mexico in his Heart

One particular incidence was probably decisive for Katz' life-long dedication to the history of the Mexican Revolution and of Mexican diplomacy: With his return to Europe turning out to be a disappointment both in Austria and in the German Democratic Republic, the following special moment in his Mexican exile may have played an important role. Friedrich Katz kept a vivid memory of it:

---

[17] Egon Erwin Kisch, *Der Fall des Generalstabschefs Redl. Außenseiter der Gesellschaft. Die Verbrechen der Gegenwart*, Verlag Die Schmiede, Berlin 1924.

"When Germany occupied the whole of France, Gilberto Bosques and all members of the consulate were detained for over two years in the German town of Bad Godesberg, where they lived in total isolation. After they had finally been exchanged for German agents and could return to Mexico in 1944, thousands of refugees congregated to welcome them. I remember that on the night of Bosques' arrival my parents took me to the Buenavista train station in Mexico. Thousands of us waited many hours for Bosques' arrival, staying in the station until the train was announced at last. When Bosques arrived, those who owed him their lives gave him a triumphal welcome."[18]

Because of his humanist attitude and political conviction, Gilberto Bosques served in the Mexican diplomatic corps as one of the protagonists of the Mexican Revolution. In occupied France he supported the antifascist resistance as Mexican consul, saved thousands of Spanish Civil War fighters in search of refuge and defended the interests of the displaced and oppressed. His political engagement was not the product of any tactical considerations, but of the principles of the Mexican Revolution, and it must have touched Friedrich Katz. He and Bosques shared a life-long friendship and the highest mutual esteem. Was it thanks to this friendship that Katz original perception of the "emigrants' ghetto" would change in later years? In the preface to the publication *Exilio y cultura. El exilio cultural austriaco en México*, Katz summarized his connection with Mexico as follows:

"For me personally, my youth in Mexico and the cordiality with which we were taken in by the Mexican people have moulded my life in many decisive ways. Even after my return to Austria Mexico has remained my spiritual home, because my entire research, my academic work, has had to with Mexico in one way or another."[19]

And so the life of Friedrich Katz confirms a quote from another Jewish exile from Vienna, who also found her real home in Mexico. Ruth Deutsch Lechuga, a medical doctor, photographer and ethnologist, summed up her emigration experience in words that seem to include that of Friedrich Katz: "In Mexico we were not treated as second-class human beings. We could move freely and develop according to our potential."[20]

---

[18] Katz, Friedrich: Unserer Familie hat die mexikanische Politik das Leben gerettet, in: Dokumentationsarchiv des österreichischen Widerstandes (ed.): *Österreicher im Exil. Mexiko 1938–1947. Eine Dokumentation*, DÖW, Wien 2002, 9-12, here 11 [my translation].

[19] Katz, Friedrich: Prólogo, in: Kloyber, Christian (ed.): *Exilio y cultura. El exilio cultural austriaco en México*, SRE, México, D.F. 2002, 15-18, here 18 [my translation].

[20] In a conversation with Christian Kloyber in Mexico in 2006.

Der Weltenläufer: Friedrich Katz und die historiographischen Debatten seiner Zeit

David Mayer

Wenige Historiker gab es im 20. Jahrhundert, die in ihrer Biographie und in ihrem Werk so viele unterschiedliche Welten miteinander verbanden wie Friedrich Katz. Während die meisten Historiker und Historikerinnen bis Ende der 1990er Jahre in völliger und heiliger Ehe mit dem Konzept der Nation lebten, verknüpfte Katz kosmopolitische Weltläufigkeit mit mehreren Wahlheimaten. „Wahlheimat", im Spanischen „patria adoptiva", fand sich auch im Titel eines mexikanischen Symposiums, das 2007 mit großem medialen Interesse und offiziellen Ehren zum 80. Geburtstag von Friedrich Katz abgehalten wurde.[1] Mexiko war indes nicht seine einzige Wahlheimat. Zu nennen wären weiters: Chicago, Ort seiner wissenschaftlichen und akademischen Arbeit seit den 1970er Jahren, Wien, das Ziel regelmäßiger und langer Besuche bis ins hohe Lebensalter sowie Ost-Berlin, beinahe 15 Jahre lang Stätte seiner abschließenden wissenschaftlichen Ausbildung und Reifung. Augenfällig ist bei alledem, dass Katz die bestimmenden globalhistorischen Bruchlinien des 20. Jahrhunderts überschritt: Ost und West, Nord und Süd. Multiple Übertritte, die in der Nachbetrachtung leichtläufig erscheinen, in ihrem Moment aber oft genug von Zwängen und Pressionen unterschiedlicher Art begleitet waren.

Dieses Grenzgehende drückte sich freilich nicht nur biographisch oder in Katz' Vielsprachigkeit aus, sondern auch in seinem geschichtswissenschaftlichem Werk. Katz verband eine breite Palette von historiographischen Perspektiven und „Stilen", auch hier die tiefen Bruchlinien des Fachs überschreitend: einen empathischen Humanismus und eine starke Sensibilität für die Ansinnen und Hoffnungen jener, die dazu verurteilt waren, nicht viele hegen zu dürfen; von konzeptuellen Kategorien und sozialgeschichtlichen Fragen geleitete Sekundäranalyse in Makroperspektive; eine tiefe Verwurzelung in empirischer Arbeit sowie eine ausgeprägte historizistische Neigung zu Forschung mit Primärquellen; die geschichtspolitische Reflexion über den gesellschaftlichen Umgang mit Geschichte; die Biographie als eines der zentralen, aber auch frag-

[1] Vgl. folgende Fest-/Gedenkschrift, die diese und zwei weitere Tagungen zu Friedrich Katz dokumentiert: Garciadiego, Javier/Kourí, Emilio (Hg.): *Revolución y exilio en la historia de México. Del amor de un historiador a su patria adoptiva: Homenaje a Friedrich Katz*, ERA/University of Chicago/El Colegio de México, México, D.F./Chicago 2010.

würdigsten Genres der Geschichtsschreibung; nicht zuletzt die marxistisch inspirierte Geschichtswissenschaft. Von letzterer zeigte sich Katz in ihren beiden großen Varianten angestoßen (eine Offenheit, die man im 20. Jahrhundert selten findet): dem Studium sozialer Strukturen (Arbeits-, Eigentums- und Klassenverhältnissen) einerseits sowie dem Interesse für *agency* andererseits, also für die Fähigkeit von einzelnen und kollektiven Akteuren, zu handeln und in den historischen Prozess zu intervenieren.

Den Reiz des Katz'schen Werks macht die Präsenz dieser unterschiedlichen Gesichtspunkte und Stile der Geschichtsschreibung aus. Auch wenn diese im gesamten Werk erkennbar werden, lassen sich die jeweiligen Perspektiven mit einigem Mut zur Vereinfachung mit unterschiedlichen biographischen Momenten und wissenschaftlichen Phasen in der Vita Friedrich Katz' in Verbindung bringen. Diese Parallelen in intellektuellem Werk und Biographie werde ich in den folgenden Überlegungen anleuchten.

Den Anfang machen der empathische Humanismus sowie die starke Sensibilität Katz' für jene, die angeblich zu Hoffnungslosigkeit verurteilt sind. Dies bildet einen diskreten, aber bedeutenden Hintergrund in einem Werk, das durch seinen nüchternen und unaufgeregten Ton gekennzeichnet ist. Eine Empathie, die sich als wichtigstes intellektuelles Erbe von Friedrich Katz' Vater, dem Journalisten, politischen Aktivisten und Schriftsteller Leo Katz (1892–1954) ansehen lässt. 1892 in der Bukowina an der multiethnischen Peripherie der k.u.k-Monarchie geboren, stieß er nach Ende des Ersten Weltkriegs zu den Kommunisten. Besonders das Zusammengehen der Verheißung radikaler Emanzipation mit einem kosmopolitischen Internationalismus, wie er für die frühe Kommunistische Internationale (Komintern) kennzeichnend war, übte starke Anziehungskraft auf ihn aus. Neben verschiedenen redaktionellen Beschäftigungen bei kommunistischen Periodika in Wien und Berlin war Leo Katz später auch als Emissär der Komintern tätig: unter anderem führte er das Doppelleben eines Waffenhändlers im Auftrag der bedrohten spanischen Republik. Wie viele zentraleuropäische Linksintellektuelle mit jüdischem Hintergrund dieser Zeit verband Leo Katz seine politische Parteinahme mit der kulturell wesentlich länger zurückreichenden Linie eines schwärmerischen Utopismus und Messianismus. Michael Löwy hat diese „Wahlverwandtschaft" als zentralen Faktor der europäischen intellektuellen Kultur vom Ende des 19. Jahrhunderts bis in die 1940er Jahre beschrieben.[2] Es ist kein Zufall, dass Leo Katz – der zunächst

[2] Löwy, Michael: *Redemption and Utopia. Jewish Libertarian Thought in Central Europe. A Study in Elective Affinity*, Athlone Press, London 1992.

journalistisch publiziert hatte und im New Yorker Exil ab 1938 schriftstellerisch zu arbeiten begann – engen und freundschaftlichen Kontakt zu Ernst Bloch pflegte. Seine Erzählungen und Romane, die sich später auch an Kinder richteten, thematisierten immer wieder jene historischen Kämpfe, die gegen übermächtige Ungerechtigkeit ausgefochten wurden, von Beginn an aussichtslos erschienen, dennoch gleichermaßen unvermeidlich waren wie sie Hoffnung boten. In diesem Doppel aus Optimismus und Melancholie blieb Leo Katz seit den 1940er Jahren angesichts der Zumutungen des Stalinismus in gewisser Weise auch persönlich gefangen.[3] Der Sohn, Friedrich Katz, nahm jedenfalls diese Sensibilität für die non-Vanitas des zum Scheitern verurteilten Aufbegehrens auf. Sie bildeten eine wichtige Inspirationsquelle in seinen Arbeiten über Agrarbewegungen in Mexiko[4] oder in seiner Pancho Villa Biographie.[5]

Zur zweiten Perspektive, die von konzeptuellen Kategorien und sozialgeschichtlichen Fragen geleitete Sekundäranalyse in Makroperspektive: Nach Kindheit und Jugend im Exil (zunächst in Paris, dann in New York, ab 1940 in Mexiko-Stadt) begann Friedrich Katz ein Universitätsstudium in New York. Dem folgten Studien in Mexiko-Stadt (1948 bis 1949 an der ENAH – Escuela Nacional de Antropología e Historia), ab 1949 in Wien. Dort schloss er 1954 seine Dissertation über *Probleme der sozialen, wirtschaftlichen und militärischen Organisation der Azteken* ab.[6] Bei dieser Arbeit handelt es sich um eine sekundäranalytische Untersuchung, die unter Verwendung eines breiten Repertoires sozio-ökonomischer Kategorien eine Synthese der Sozialgeschichte des alten Mesoamerikas anzubieten versuchte. Ein Vorgehen, das aus heutiger Sicht

[3] Zu Leo Katz vgl.: Mayer, David: Leo Katz (1892–1954): viele Welten in einer Welt, in: Hausberger, Bernd (Hg.): *Globale Lebensläufe. Menschen als Akteure im weltgeschichtlichen Geschehen*, Mandelbaum, Wien 2006, 233-256.

[4] Vgl.: Katz, Friedrich: *Riot, Rebellion, and Revolution. Rural social conflict in Mexico*, Princeton University Press, Princeton u.a. 1988.

[5] Vgl.: Katz, Friedrich: *The Life and Times of Pancho Villa*, Stanford University Press, Stanford 1998.

[6] Veröffentlicht in Deutsch in der DDR, später auch auf Spanisch in Mexiko: Katz, Friedrich: *Die sozialökonomischen Verhältnisse bei den Azteken im 15. und 16. Jahrhundert*, Deutscher Verlag d. Wissenschaften, Berlin 1956. Katz, Friedrich: *Situación social y económica de los aztecas durante los siglos XV y XVI*, Universidad Nacional Autónoma de México/Instituto de Investigaciones Históricas, México, D.F. 1966. Ein darauf aufbauendes Überblickswerk zu den altamerikanischen Kulturen insgesamt erschien 1969 in Westdeutschland: Katz, Friedrich: *Vorkolumbische Kulturen. Die großen Reiche des alten Amerika*, Kindler, München 1969.

unspektakulär und herkömmlich erscheinen mag, sich Anfang der 1950er Jahre aber noch in der Pionierzone der gerade erst ihren Aufstieg beginnenden Sozialgeschichte befand. Der Text ist auf Systematik und Synthese konzentriert, die marxistische Inspiration wird nicht zur Schau gestellt oder dogmatisch deklamiert. So finden sich z. B. keine Zitate der marxistischen „Klassiker“. Diese zurückhaltende Fundierung des Marxismus – unter jenen, die in der zweiten Hälfte des 20. Jahrhunderts im Westen und im Süden den unterschiedlichen Linien marxistischer Historiographie zuzurechnen waren, ein eher seltenes Vorgehen – sollte auch später typisch für das Katz'sche Werk bleiben. Trotz dieser Zurückhaltung musste Katz in Wien eine offene Ablehnung seiner Perspektive und seiner Arbeit erfahren. Und zwar aus unverhohlen politischen Gründen: Die am Institut für Völkerkunde angesiedelten Betreuer seiner Doktorarbeit teilten ihm mit, dass man ihm einzig für die DDR eine Empfehlung schreiben könne.[7] Wie Katz in einem Interview nicht ohne Bitterkeit anmerkte: „Mit anderen Worten, man hat mich rausgeschmissen aus Österreich. Hitler hat's das erste Mal getan und Heine-Geldern tat das das zweite Mal.“[8] Der Umzug Katz' nach Ost-Berlin im Februar 1956 war also die Folge der erstickenden intellektuellen Enge und Kleingeistigkeit, die in Österreich in den 1950er Jahren vorherrschte.

Die Jahre in der DDR, Land der Hoffnungen, aber auch der Desillusionierung für Katz, waren nicht nur äußerst fruchtbar, sondern spielten eine wesentlich bedeutendere Rolle in seiner intellektuellen Entwicklung als gemeinhin anerkannt wird. Von 1956 an arbeitete Katz am Institut für Allgemeine Geschichte (Abteilung Geschichte der Neuzeit) der Humboldt-Universität zu Berlin, bis zu seiner Habilitierung 1963 als wissenschaftlicher Aspirant bzw. Oberassistent,

---

[7] Katz war laut selbstverfasstem und im Personalakt an der Humboldt-Universität zu Berlin abgelegtem Lebenslauf seit 1949 Mitglied der Kommunistischen Partei Österreichs (KPÖ) sowie der Vereinigung demokratischer Studenten Österreichs. Universitätsarchiv der Humboldt-Universität zu Berlin, Personalakte K 1102, Prof. Dr. Friedrich Katz (=UA HUB Personalakt Katz), Lebenslauf von Friedrich Katz, nicht datiert (ca. 1965), Blatt 7-10.

[8] Interview mit Friedrich Katz, Wien 17.12.2007. Robert Heine-Geldern (1885–1968) spielte seit seiner Rückkehr aus dem US-amerikanischen Exil 1950 eine maßgebliche Rolle am Institut für Völkerkunde der Universität Wien und zeichnete als Zweitbetreuer von Katz' Dissertation. Die Erstbetreuung hatte Wilhelm Koppers inne. Vgl. auch den Beitrag von Martina Kaller in diesem Band über *Friedrich Katz an der Universität Wien. Von der Exzellenz ins Nichts.*

von 1963 bis 1966 als Dozent. Im September 1966 wurde er zum „Professor mit Lehrauftrag“ ernannt, 1969 zum „ordentlichen Professor“.[9]

In der DDR war Katz auch als Simultanübersetzer bei Kongressen und ähnlichen Veranstaltungen tätig. Dabei teilte er, wie er im Interview erzählte, seine Kabine immer wieder mit einer Deutschen, die späterhin an der Seite von Che Guevara im bolivianischen Regenwald kämpfen und unter dem Namen *Tania la Guerrillera* berühmt werden sollte: Tamara Bunke (1933–1967).[10] Die mit Lateinamerika verbundenen Milieus in der DDR waren jedenfalls klein. Neben den wenigen Forschern und einigen Funktionären mit Lateinamerikabezug pflegte Katz engen Kontakt mit den „Mexikanern“, also kommunistischen Parteigängern, die während des Nationalsozialismus in Mexiko Exil gefunden, in den 1950er Jahren in der DDR jedoch Verfolgung und Marginalisierung erlitten (Paul Merker, Walter Janka u.a.).

Eine wichtige Rolle unter Katz’ Kontakten spielte der Leipziger Historiker Walter Markov (1909–1993).[11] Dieser arbeitete zwar selbst nicht zu Lateinamerika – Markov sollte mit seinen Studien zu den radikalen plebejischen Strömungen in der Französischen Revolution bekannt werden – hatte aber Anfang der 1960er Jahre versucht, in der DDR ein Forschungsprogramm für vergleichende Kolonialgeschichte zu etablieren. Markov, wie Katz ursprünglich aus Österreich stammend, war einer der kreativen und intellektuell fundiertesten Historiker der DDR. Während für andere der Marxismus nur eine äußerliche Pflicht blieb, vertrat Markov wissenschaftlich und politisch einen „integralen

---

[9] Vgl. die entsprechenden Ernennungsurkunden und Dienstzeitenaufstellungen in: UA HUB Personalakt Katz. Interessant sind im Personalakt insbesondere jene Korrespondenzen, die neben einer Beurteilung von Katz auch einen Antrag auf Verlängerung der Aspirantur enthalten. Sie führen eine Vielzahl von Aktivitäten von Katz in Forschung, Lehre und politischer Publizistik an, die die Verzögerung des Habilitationsabschlusses begründen: So heißt es in einem Schreiben von 1959, dass Katz u.a. zum Putsch gegen die Regierung Árbenz in Guatemala 1954 und zu lateinamerikanischen Befreiungsbewegungen Vorträge hielt und Artikel für universitätsinterne Publikationen verfasste. Vgl. UA HUB Personalakt Katz, Schreiben von F. Katz vom 1.12.1959 an das Prorektorat für den wissenschaftlichen Nachwuchs betr. Verlängerung der Aspirantur bis Ende 1960 (gez. von F. Katz und G. Schilfert), Blatt 60.

[10] Interview mit Friedrich Katz, Wien 17.12.2007.

[11] Zu Leben und Werk von Walter Markov siehe u.a.: Neuhaus, Manfred/Seidel, Helmut/Diesener, Gerald/Middell, Matthias (Hg.): *Wenn jemand seinen Kopf bewusst hinhielt... Beiträge zu Werk und Wirken von Walter Markov,* Rosa-Luxemburg-Stiftung Sachsen, Leipzig 1998^2. Markov, Walter: *Wie viele Leben lebt der Mensch. Eine Autobiographie aus dem Nachlaß*, Faber & Faber, Leipzig 2009.

Marxismus“, der, ähnlich wie die französische *Annales*-Schule, eine Synthese der verschiedenen Dimensionen des Gesellschaftlichen forderte. Damit bot Markov Katz nicht nur thematisch und perspektivisch einen interessanten Rahmen, sondern auch intellektuell. Darüber hinaus arbeitete der wichtigste Schüler Markovs, Manfred Kossok (1930–1993), der gleichen Generation angehörig wie Katz, auch zu Lateinamerika. Die freundschaftliche Verbindung zwischen Katz und Kossok sollte bis zu Kossoks frühem Tod 1993 währen. Sie war, insbesondere nachdem Markov und Kossok Anfang der 1970er Jahre ein weit über die Grenzen der DDR hinaus bekanntes Forschungsprogramm zur vergleichenden Revolutionsgeschichte begründet hatten,[12] von vielen gemeinsamen Aktivitäten begleitet. In den 1960er Jahren jedenfalls bildete der Kreis von Markov, Kossok, Katz (später gesellte sich noch der mexikanische Historiker Enrique Semo hinzu),[13] einen wichtigen, wenn nicht den wichtigsten Knotenpunkt der historiographischen Forschungen und offenen Diskussionen zu Lateinamerika in der DDR.

Im Jahr 1964 wurde Katz' Habilitation über *Deutschland, Diaz und die mexikanische Revolution. Die deutsche Politik in Mexiko 1870–1920* veröffentlicht.[14] In dieser wird der dritte Zug im historiographischen Werk von Friedrich Katz deutlich sichtbar: seine ausgeprägte Neigung zu Forschung mit Primärquellen und die historizistische Fundierung seiner Arbeit in der quellenbasierten Rekonstruktion des historischen Prozesses. Diese Habilitationsschrift war nicht nur von Markov betreut worden, sondern ließ auch dessen Einfluss deutlich erkennbar werden: Denn Markov hatte seine eigene Habilitation über die Geschichte der deutschen Balkandiplomatie verfasst (approbiert 1947) und darin

[12] Zur vergleichenden Revolutionsgeschichte in Leipzig siehe z. B.: Middell, Matthias: *Weltgeschichtsschreibung im Zeitalter der Verfachlichung und Professionalisierung.* Vol. 3: *Von der vergleichenden Kulturgeschichte zur Revolutionskomparatistik*, Akademische Verlagsanstalt, Leipzig 2005. Mayer, David: Transnationale Debattengeflechte in marxistisch inspirierten Historiographien: Die Übergangsdebatten und ihre Rezeption in der DDR, in: Steidl, Annemarie et al. (Hg.): *Übergänge und Schnittmengen. Arbeit, Migration, Bevölkerung und Wissenschaftsgeschichte in Diskussion*, Böhlau, Wien 2008, 284-289.

[13] Enrique Semo (* 1930) absolvierte 1968 bis 1971 sein Doktoratsstudium an der Humboldt-Universität. In seiner Dissertation, betreut von Manfred Kossok, ging es um die *Die ökonomischen Ursprünge der mexikanischen Nation (1521–1759).* Zu den intensiven Kontakten zwischen Semo, Katz und Kossok vgl. den Nachruf: Semo, Enrique: Friedrich Katz, in: http://mexicanstudies.uchicago.edu/page/essays#semo (Zugriff 06.04.2012).

[14] Katz, Friedrich: *Deutschland, Diaz und die mexikanische Revolution. Die deutsche Politik in Mexiko 1870–1920* (=Schriftenreihe des Instituts für Allgemeine Geschichte an der Humboldt-Universität Berlin 9), Deutscher Verlag d. Wissenschaften, Berlin 1964.

mit einem herkömmlichen diplomatiegeschichtlichen Forschungsdesign, also dem Studium der Akten in den offiziellen Archiven des Außenministeriums und seiner analogen Vorgängerbehörden, Fragen diskutiert, die über eine übliche Diplomatiegeschichte weit hinausgingen.[15] Fragen des Zusammenspiels unterschiedlicher Akteure und der, wie man heute sagen würde, „Verflechtung" historischer Prozesse an unterschiedlichen Orten, Fragen der ökonomischen Abhängigkeit sowie Fragen der Asymmetrie und ihrer symbolisch-diskursiven Untermauerung. Analog ging Katz nun in Bezug auf die Politik Deutschlands gegenüber Mexiko vor und es ist auch dieses Prozedere einer über die Diplomatiegeschichte hinausgehenden Diplomatiegeschichte, das ihn Anfang der 1980er Jahre mit seiner erweiterten Studie über die Großmachtpolitik gegenüber Mexiko während der Revolution berühmt machen sollte. Das Geheimnis von *The Secret War*[16] findet sich nicht zuletzt in jenem Ost-Berlin bzw. Leipzig der 1960er Jahren, wo sich im realen Sozialismus ein Milieu eines kritisch reflektierten Marxismus etabliert hatte.[17]

Das Jahr 1968 wurde zu einem wichtigen Wendepunkt für Katz – in seiner Biographie überschneiden sich zwei Schauplätze des „globalen 1968":[18] Osteuropa und, wie man heute weiß, das Ende der Hoffnungen auf eine Rekonstituierung des realen Sozialismus aus sich heraus; und Lateinamerika, besonders Mexiko, wo im Kontext der langen, von der Kubanischen Revolution befeuerten 1960er Jahre Schüler, Studierende und in Ansätzen auch andere Bevölkerungsteile die Versprechen der Mexikanischen Revolution auf Freiheit und soziale Gerechtigkeit für sich neu belebten und von den offiziellen Gralshütern dieser Revolution, der Staatspartei PRI, dafür mit blutiger Repression zum Schweigen gebracht wurden. Mit Blick auf Osteuropa und die DDR zog Katz die Konsequenz aus der Ernüchterung und nutzte das Privileg eines westlichen Passes, um das Land 1970 mit seiner Familie zu verlassen. An der Humboldt-Universität hatte man seine Stelle noch im September 1969, nur zwei Jahre nach Beginn seiner Anwartsprofessur in eine volle Professur umgewan-

---

[15] Markov, Walter: *Grundzüge der Balkandiplomatie. Ein Beitrag zur Geschichte der Abhängigkeitsverhältnisse*, Leipziger Universitäts-Verlag, Leipzig 1999.

[16] Katz, Friedrich: *The Secret War in Mexico. Europe, the United States and the Mexican revolution*, University of Chicago Press, Chicago u.a. 1981.

[17] Ein Milieu, das sich freilich einer Reihe von Verfolgungen und Pressionen ausgesetzt sah. So war z. B. Markov 1951 des Titoismus beschuldigt und aus der SED ausgeschlossen worden.

[18] Vgl.: Kastner, Jens/Mayer, David (Hg.): *Weltwende 1968? Ein Jahr aus globalgeschichtlicher Perspektive*, Mandelbaum, Wien 2008.

delt. Dies lässt sich als Zeichen dafür werten, dass man Katz an der Humboldt-Universität zu halten versuchte. Nach verschiedenen Gastprofessuren fand er im Jahr 1971 eine neue Wirkungsstätte an der University of Chicago, einer gleichermaßen renommierten wie im Ruf konservativer Vorherrschaft stehenden Eliteschule. Mit Blick auf Mexiko wurde Katz im Laufe der 1970er Jahre Teil jenes Öffnungsprozesses, der nach dem Massaker an Studierenden am Platz der Drei Kulturen zumindest akademisch vonstatten ging und gerade in der geschichtspolitisch äußerst brisanten Historiographie der Mexikanischen Revolution eine Pluralisierung der Stimmen und Interpretationen bedeutete.

Die Welle neuer, „revisionistischer" Interpretationen der Mexikanischen Revolution, die Ende der 1960er, Anfang der 1970er Jahre anhob, brachte einerseits sozialgeschichtlich ausgerichtete Studien, andererseits Deutungen mit einer Perspektive „von unten". Zudem handelte es sich bei vielen dieser Arbeiten um offen engagierte Interpretationen, denen es darum ging, die als unerledigt betrachteten „Aufgaben" der Mexikanischen Revolution neu anzugehen. Autoren wie der US-Amerikaner John Womack, der aus Argentinien stammende Aktivist Adolfo Gilly und der Mexikaner Arnaldo Córdova machten den Anfang, viele andere folgten.[19] Nicht-mexikanische Historiker spielten dabei eine wichtige Rolle. Zu ihnen zählte auch Friedrich Katz, der ab Mitte der 1970er Jahre mit kürzeren sozialgeschichtlichen Arbeiten publizistisch in Mexiko präsent wurde und Anfang der 1980er Jahre mit seinem *The Secret War* jene Arbeit vorlegte, die auch in die breitere Öffentlichkeit wirken sollte und deren Ruhm ihn bis zu seinem Lebensende begleitete.

Katz bezog die politischen Implikationen von Geschichtsschreibung, insbesondere der Geschichte von Revolutionen, aufmerksam in seine Arbeit ein. Mit Blick auf den umfassenden Erfolg der revisionistischen Interpretationen der Mexikanischen Revolution der 1970er Jahre[20] bemerkte Katz: Die Regierung hatte „das Gefühl, dass wir der Revolution eine gewisse Legitimierung im Ausland und Inland

---

[19] Womack Jr., John: *Zapata and the Mexican Revolution*, Knopf, New York 1969. Córdova, Arnaldo: *La ideología de la revolución mexicana. La formación del nuevo régimen*, ERA, México, D.F. 1973. Gilly, Adolfo: *La revolución interrumpida. México 1910–1920: Una guerra campesina por la tierra y el pod*er, El Caballito, México D.F. 1971.

[20] Dieser Revisionismus war in hohem Maße von marxistischen Interpretationen inspiriert, während sich die zur gleichen Zeit aufkommenden revisionistischen Interpretationen der Englischen oder Französischen Revolution als Kritik an der Vorherrschaft marxistischer Deutungen etablierten. Zur Vielgestaltigkeit von Revisionismen in der Historiographie vgl.: Traverso, Enzo: *Gebrauchsanleitungen für die Vergangenheit. Geschichte, Erinnerung, Politik*, Unrast, Münster 2007, 95-99.

geschaffen haben. Keiner von uns hat natürlich behauptet, dass die PRI die Nachfolgerin der Revolution sei. Aber indem wir [...] die Mexikanische Revolution als Revolution bezeichnet haben, was ja die Konservativen leugneten, sind wir automatisch akzeptiert worden. Das war eben das Wichtige."[21] Diese widersprüchliche Gemengelage aus weit reichender Delegitimierung der PRI-Regierung ob ihrer Nichterfüllung revolutionärer Versprechen und der historiographischen Fundierung des zentralen geschichtspolitischen Anspruchs dieser Regierung – nämlich, dass sie aus einer authentischen Revolution (und nicht einem sinnlosen Blutvergießen) hervorgegangen war – bestimmte den eigentümlichen Charakter der verschiedenen Neuinterpretationen seit den 1970er Jahren.

Katz kannte jedoch nicht nur die geschichtspolitischen Verwicklungen in Bezug auf den mexikanischen Staat, sondern auch die politisch wie intellektuell komplex gelagerten Schichten der in diesen neuen Interpretationen zunächst tonangebenden marxistischen Kategorien. Katz verfolgte dabei seinen eigenen Weg einer zurückhaltenden und ruhigen Anknüpfung an den Marxismus. Wo mit starker Hitze und in Form eines unmittelbaren innerlinken Strömungskampfes diskutiert wurde – wie in einem Sammelband zur Mexikanischen Revolution, in dem kommunistische, trotzkistische, gramscianische und maoistische Interpretationen in Wettstreit traten[22] –, fand man Katz nicht. Genauso wenig intervenierte er in die in den 1970er Jahre allgemein virulente Debatte über „Feudalismus" und „Kapitalismus" in der Geschichte Lateinamerikas in theoretischer oder begriffsableitender Manier (was damals weit verbreitet war), sondern in einer konkret sozialgeschichtlichen: Ihn interessierte der Charakter der vorrevolutionären Haziendas in Mexiko und ihrer unfreien Arbeitsverhältnisse (Schuldknechtschaft etc.), also die Frage, ob es sich bei den Haziendas um eine vormoderne Agrarinstitution gehandelt habe, deren Besitzer vom Motiv des „Prestiges" angetrieben waren, oder ob die Haziendas als moderne kapitalistische Unternehmen anzusehen seien, deren Grundlage die Logik der Kapitalakkumulation war.[23] Der Fokus der Katz'schen Veröffentlichungen in den 1970er Jahren war jedenfalls ein markant agrar- und sozialgeschichtlicher.

---

[21] Interview mit Friedrich Katz, Wien 17.12.2007.

[22] Gilly, Adolfo/Córdova, Arnaldo/Bartra, Armando/Aguilar Mora, Manuel/Semo, Enrique: *Interpretaciones de la Revolución Mexicana*, Nueva Imagen, México, D.F. 1989[12] (1979).

[23] Katz, Friedrich: Condiciones de trabajo en las haciendas de México durante el porfiriato: modalidades y tendencias, in: Katz, Friedrich (Hg.): *La servidumbre agraria en México en la época porfiriana* (=SepSetentas Bd. 303), Secretaría de Educación Pública, México, D.F. 1976, 15-91. Katz, Friedrich: El campesinado en la revolución mexicana de 1910, in: *El Trimestre Económico* 1/4 (1976), 118-134.

Von einer anderen, weit verbreiteten marxistischen Debatte der 1970er Jahre – jener über die Produktionsweisen im kolonialen Lateinamerika – hielt sich Katz fern. Wie er im Interview meinte: „Da wollt' ich gar nicht einsteigen, das war mir zu esoterisch."[24] Größeres Interesse hegte Katz dagegen für die Auseinandersetzungen über die so genannte Asiatische Produktionsweise und die Anwendung dieses Konzepts auf die präkolumbischen Gesellschaften. In Mexiko hatte diese Diskussion einige wichtige Proponenten wie Angel Palerm, Roger Bartra, Pedro Carrasco oder Johanna Broda. Katz teilte mit den Genannten die aufmerksame Kenntnis der klassischen Schrift von Karl Wittfogel über *Die orientalische Despotie* sowie seiner These von der Bedeutung von Wasserinfrastrukturen für die vormoderne Zivilisationen (hydraulische Gesellschaften).[25] Katz' Interesse an diesen Diskussionen war jedoch weniger von „amerikanischen" als von „osteuropäischen" Gesichtspunkten angestoßen: Während in Lateinamerika die Spezifik der Zivilisationen der Azteken, Maya und Inka im Mittelpunkt stand, versuchten osteuropäische Intellektuelle bei der Wiederentdeckung des in den 1930er Jahren unter Stalin verdrängten Konzepts „Asiatische Produktionsweise" den realen Sozialismus analytisch auf den Punkt zu bringen: Da sich der Begriff bei Marx auf Gesellschaften ohne Privateigentum, aber mit einem allmächtigen, die Wirtschaft zentral verwaltenden Staat bezogen hatte, müsste doch der reale Sozialismus mit diesem Begriff zu beschreiben sein.[26] Die gleiche Diskussion im weltweiten Geflecht marxistisch inspirierter Debatten, jedoch mit jeweils eigenen Hintergründen und Motiven – Katz erwies sich als einer der wenigen, der mit diesen beiden unterschiedlichen Kontexten biographisch und intellektuell verbunden war.

Katz integrierte in seine Arbeit auch den zweiten großen Strang marxistisch inspirierter Geschichtsanalyse: das Interesse für die *agency*, insbesondere der Bevölkerungsmehrheit, der im klassischen „Archiv" meist die unmittelbare Stimme fehlt. Die Fähigkeit zu Handeln und Intervention interessierte Katz sowohl bei Kollektiven – siehe seine bereits erwähnten Arbeiten über Agrarbewegungen – als auch bei Individuen – siehe sein letztes großes Werk über die

---

[24] Interview mit Friedrich Katz, Wien 17.12.2007.

[25] Wittfogel, Karl August: *Die orientalische Despotie. Eine vergleichende Untersuchung totaler Macht*, Kiepenheuer & Witsch, Köln 1962. Wittfogel, Karl August: *The Hydraulic Civilizations*, University of Chicago Press, Chicago 1956.

[26] Zur wechselhaften Geschichte der Diskussion um die Asiatische Produktionsweise vgl.: O'Leary, Brendan: *The Asiatic Mode of Production. Oriental Despotism, Historical Materialism and Indian History* (with a foreword by Ernest Gellner), Basil Blackwell, Oxford u.a. 1989.

legendäre Führungsfigur der Mexikanischen Revolution im Norden des Landes, Francisco „Pancho" Villa.[27] Gerade dieser Hintergrund des marxistisch inspirierten Interesses für sozial eingebettete *agency* verleiht Katz in *The Life and Times of Pancho Villa* die Fähigkeit, die Untiefen des biographischen Genres zu umgehen – unangemessene Psychologisierung, Individualisierung, teleologische Unterstellung eines „Lebensmusters", Heldenkitsch – und diesen mythenbeladenen, jedenfalls sehr facettenreichen und ambivalenten Akteur kritisch darzustellen. Zugleich vermag Katz die unbestreitbaren Vorteile des biographischen Genres – der Farbreichtum einer erzählenden, nicht nur analytischen Rekonstruktion, die Aufmerksamkeit für das Detail und eine gewisse Empathie für den (Anti-)Helden – zu wahren. Es sind das Leben *und* die Zeit des Pancho Villa, es sind Analyse *und* Erzählung und es ist die Inspiration durch marxistische Kategorien, ohne dass diese im Text auftrumpfen würden, die dieses späte Werk auszeichnen.

Friedrich Katz verband in seinem Werk äußerst unterschiedliche Wege und Stile der historiographischen Arbeit. Dies gelang im 20. Jahrhundert nicht häufig. Dabei spielte der in seinen Schriften vernehmbare, von Gelassenheit gekennzeichnete Ton eine wichtige Rolle. Dies ist umso bemerkenswerter, als z. B. die Debatten über die Mexikanische Revolution Anfang der 1970er Jahre in einem Ton alarmistischer Unmittelbarkeit und äußerster Dringlichkeit ausgetragen wurden – das Herzrasen der Revolution, die zu dieser Zeit von Aktivisten und Aktivistinnen als erneut imminent wahrgenommen wurde, ist in ihnen deutlich spürbar. Katz' Arbeiten, denen es nicht an Empathie und Leidenschaft mangelt, strahlen dagegen Ruhe und Umsicht aus. Seine Botschaft scheint zu lauten: es handelt sich um eine Revolution, gewiss, dies ist aber kein Grund sich verrückt machen zu lassen. Für Maß und Proportionen, grundlegend für jede Historiographie, hatte Katz einen ausnehmend scharfen Sinn.

[27] Katz, Friedrich: *The Life and Times of Pancho Villa*, Stanford University Press, Stanford 1998.

Well-Versed in Worlds: Friedrich Katz and the historiographical debates of his time

David Mayer

There are probably few twentieth century historians who will bear comparison with Friedrich Katz for being, in their life and in their work, so well-versed in so many different worlds. At a time – right up to the late 1990s – when almost the whole profession was practically married to the idea of the "nation-state", Katz combined his cosmopolitanism with ties to several adopted homelands. Adopted homelands, "patria adoptiva" in Spanish, quite appropriately featured in the title of a 2007 conference in Mexico in honour of Friedrich Katz' 80th birthday; this conference involved high-ranking officials and evoked a great deal of interest from the media.[1] Mexico was however far from being Katz' only adopted home: there was also Chicago, where he engaged in scholarly and academic work from the 1970s onward; Vienna to which he used to pay regular and lengthy visits right up to the end of his life; and East Berlin, where he concluded his academic training, reached maturity as a scholar, and made his home for almost 15 years. What is remarkable about all this is the apparent ease with which Katz commuted across the seemingly all-important fault lines of twentieth century global history: East and West, North and South. The smoothness with which, in retrospect, Katz seems to have performed these multiple border crossings is of course illusory; more often than not, he found himself having to cope with a host of different constraints and pressures.

Crossing borders is a leitmotif not only in Katz' life, but also in his oeuvre as a historian. He used a broad palette of historiographical perspectives and "styles", which enabled him to transcend the deep fault lines criss-crossing the discipline: an empathetic humanism and a finely honed sensibility for the aspirations and hopes of those who were condemned to seeing many, if not all of them, dashed; a "big picture" meta-analysis guided by conceptual categories and sociohistorical questions; a rootedness in empirical work and a pronounced historicist tendency to work with primary sources; a reflectiveness on the political

[1] Cf. the commemorative *Festschrift*, which documents two other conferences in addition to the one mentioned above: Garciadiego, Javier/Kourí, Emilio (eds.): *Revolución y exilio en la historia de México. Del amor de un historiador a su patria adoptiva: Homenaje a Friedrich Katz*, ERA/University of Chicago/El Colegio de México, México, D.F./Chicago 2010.

implications and (mis-)uses of history; biography as a central and at the same time highly controversial genre of historiography; and last but not least Marxist historiography. With regard to the latter Katz was, to an extent unusual in twentieth century historians, at home with both of its great variants, the study of social structures (relations of labour, property and class) and the interest in agency, i.e., the ability of both individual and collective actors to intervene in the historical process.

What makes Katz' writings so attractive is the presence of these different historiographical styles. Although discernible in his entire oeuvre, these specific perspectives can be linked, if a certain licence for simplification is granted, to different stages in his life and to different phases of his career as a scholar. These parallels between Katz' oeuvre and his life will form the basis of this paper.

There is, first of all, Katz' empathetic humanism and his strong sympathy for those who are apparently condemned to live without hope. These form an unobtrusive, ever present undertow in an oeuvre that is marked by its sober and level-headed tone. At the same time, they are arguably the most important intellectual inheritance from his father Leo Katz (1892–1954), a journalist, political activist and author. Born in 1892 in the Bukowina at the Habsburg Empire's multiethnic north eastern periphery, Leo Katz had joined the Communists after the end of World War I. His prime motivation in taking this step seems to have been the way the Communists combined the promise of radical emancipation with the cosmopolitan internationalism prominent in the early Comintern. A member of the editorial boards of various Communist periodicals in Vienna and Berlin, Leo Katz was also to serve as a Comintern emissary and led a double life that included channeling armaments to the imperilled Spanish Republic. As was the case with many other Central European intellectuals from a Jewish background, Leo Katz' political partisanship had overtones of an enthusiastic utopian and messianic tradition with an age-old cultural lineage. Michael Löwy has described this "elective affinity" as a key factor of European intellectual life between the late nineteenth century and the 1940s.[2] Therefore it does not come as a surprise that Leo Katz, who reinvented himself as a novelist in his New York exile from 1938 on, was engaged in frequent friendly exchanges with Ernst Bloch. His stories and novels, some of them written for children, frequently revolve around those historic struggles that pitted underdogs against the vastly

---

[2] Löwy, Michael: *Redemption and Utopia. Jewish Libertarian Thought in Central Europe. A Study in Elective Affinity*, Athlone Press, London 1992.

superior forces of injustice: with no other hope in sight whatever they did, long odds could never keep the weaker side from putting up a fight. This seesaw of optimism and melancholy cast a deeply personal spell on Leo Katz from the 1940s onwards as he was faced by the atrocities committed by Stalin himself and by others acting in his name.[3] Friedrich Katz shared his father's keen appreciation of the value of rebellion in a seemingly hopeless cause. It was to be an important source of inspiration in his works on the agrarian movements in Mexico[4] and in his biography of Pancho Villa.[5]

Then there is the tool of macro perspective meta-analysis guided by conceptual categories and sociohistorical questions. Having spent his childhood and adolescence in exile (first in Paris, then in New York and from 1940 in Mexico City), Friedrich Katz began his university studies in New York and moved on to Mexico City (1948 to 1949 at the ENAH – Escuela Nacional de Antropología e Historia) and, in 1949, to Vienna. He graduated in 1954 from the University of Vienna with a doctoral thesis on *Probleme der sozialen, wirtschaftlichen und militärischen Organisation der Azteken* (*Problems of the Social, Economic and Military Organisation of the Aztecs*).[6] The thesis is a study of secondary analysis attempting to achieve, through the use of a broad repertoire of socio-economic categories, a synthesis of the social history of ancient Mesoamerica: an approach that impresses us as unspectacular or even traditional today while in the early 1950s it was still a novel addition to the methodology of social history at a time when social history itself was just beginning its rise to prominence. The text is focussed on systematics and on synthesis, the Marxist inspiration is not paraded ostentatiously or used purely for dogmatic harangues. There are for instance

---

[3] For Leo Katz cf. Mayer, David: Leo Katz (1892–1954): viele Welten in einer Welt, in: Hausberger, Bernd (ed.): *Globale Lebensläufe. Menschen als Akteure im weltgeschichtlichen Geschehen*, Mandelbaum, Wien 2006, 233-256.

[4] Cf. Katz, Friedrich: *Riot, Rebellion, and Revolution. Rural social conflict in Mexico*, Princeton University Press, Princeton et al. 1988.

[5] Cf. Katz, Friedrich: *The Life and Times of Pancho Villa*, Stanford University Press, Stanford 1998.

[6] First published in the GDR, later also in Mexico in Spanish: Katz, Friedrich: *Die sozialökonomischen Verhältnisse bei den Azteken im 15. und 16. Jahrhundert*, Deutscher Verlag d. Wissenschaften, Berlin 1956. Katz, Friedrich: *Situación social y económica de los aztecas durante los siglos XV y XVI*, Universidad Nacional Autónoma de México (Instituto de Investigaciones Históricas), México, D.F. 1966. An overview of the cultures of the ancient Americas was published in West Germany in 1969: Katz, Friedrich: *Vorkolumbische Kulturen. Die großen Reiche des alten Amerika*, Kindler, München 1969.

no quotations from Marxist "classics". This muted voicing of Marxist positions – rare enough among historians who, in the West and in the South, professed allegiance to endemic versions of Marxism – was to remain a typical feature in Katz' oeuvre. Despite his aversion to tub-thumping rhetoric Katz was to face a radical rejection of his perspective and work in Vienna – for reasons that were avowedly political: The Institut für Völkerkunde supervisors of his thesis informed him that the only place they could recommend him to was the GDR.[7] As Katz remarked, not without bitterness, in an interview, "In other words, I was thrown out of Austria twice. The first time courtesy of Hitler, the second time courtesy of Heine-Geldern."[8] Katz' move to East Berlin in February 1956 was therefore a direct result of the stifling narrow-mindedness that characterized Austria in the 1950s.

The years Katz spent in the GDR, for him a land of hope as well as of disillusionment, were not only extremely fruitful but contributed much more to his intellectual development than is commonly acknowledged. From 1956 Katz was employed as a postgraduate *wissenschaftlicher Aspirant* (later *Oberassistent*) at the Institut für Allgemeine Geschichte (Abteilung Geschichte der Neuzeit) of the Humboldt University of Berlin until his habilitation in 1963, and as a lecturer from 1963 to 1966. In September 1966 he was appointed a *Professor mit Lehrauftrag*, an associate professor, becoming a full professor in 1969.[9]

---

[7] According to a CV, apparently written by himself, which is now part of his personal file at the Humboldt University of Berlin, Katz had been a member, from 1949, of the Communist Party of Austria (KPÖ) and of the Vereinigung demokratischer Studenten Österreichs. Universitätsarchiv der Humboldt-Universität zu Berlin, Personalakte K 1102, Prof. Dr. Friedrich Katz (=UA HUB Personalakt Katz), CV Friedrich Katz, without date (c. 1965), pages 7-10.

[8] Interview with Friedrich Katz, Vienna December 17, 2007 [my translation]. Robert Heine-Geldern (1885–1968), who returned from exile in the United States in 1950, played a significant role at the Institut für Völkerkunde [Department of Ethnology] of Vienna University and was the second supervisor of Katz' thesis. The first supervisor was Wilhelm Koppers. Cf. Martina Kaller's contribution to this volume *Friedrich Katz an der Universität Wien. Von der Exzellenz ins Nichts* [*Friedrich Katz at the University of Vienna. From excellence to nothingness*].

[9] Cf. the pertinent appointment documents and lists of service times in UA HUB Personalakt Katz. Of particular interest in Katz' personal file in addition to the assessment of his work is the correspondence relating to his request to have his post-doc status [Aspirantur] prolonged. Katz' many activities in research, tuition and political journalism are mentioned as having delayed the completion of his habilitation. In a letter from 1959, Katz points out that his activities had included lectures on the coup against the Árbenz

In the GDR Katz also worked as a simultaneous interpreter at conferences and comparable events. On these occasions, as he recounted in an interview, he often shared a booth with Tamara Bunke (1933–1967), who was to join Che Guevara as a fighter in the rainforests of Bolivia and became famous as Tania la Guerrillera.[10] Groups with links to Latin America were in any case few and far between in the GDR. In addition to a handful of researchers and a few political functionaries with Latin American ties Katz was in close contact with the *Mexikaner*, members of the Communist Party who had found refuge in Mexico during the Nazi era and had returned to the GDR after the war, only to be exposed to persecution and marginalization in the 1950s (Paul Merker, Walter Janka et al.).

Among Katz' contacts a special role must be accorded to the Leipzig historian Walter Markov (1909–1993).[11] While not concerned with Latin America himself – his name came to be associated above all with studies of radical plebeian tendencies in the French Revolution – Markov had launched an attempt in the early 1960s to establish a research programme for comparative colonial history in the GDR. Markov, like Katz originally from Austria, belonged to a group of the GDR's most creative and intellectually accomplished historians. While others merely paid lip service to Marxism, Markov represented both in scholarly and political terms an "integral" version of Marxism, demanding a synthesis of different societal dimensions as typified by the French *Annales* school. This meant that Markov provided Katz with an interesting thematic, perspectival and intellectual framework. There was also Manfred Kossok (1930–1993), Markov's most promising former student: belonging to the same generation as Katz, Kossok was also working on topics related to Latin America. The friendly relationship between Katz and Kossok was terminated only by Kossok's untimely death in 1993; it bore fruit in a great number of shared activities, especially after

government in Guatemala in 1954 and on Latin American liberation movements and writing copy for University publications. Cf. UA HUB Personalakt Katz, F. Katz' letter of December 1, 1959, to the "Prorektorat für den wissenschaftlichen Nachwuchs" on the extension of his post-doctoral status [Aspirantur] until the end of 1960 (signed by F. Katz and G. Schilfert), page 60.

[10] Interview with Friedrich Katz, Vienna, December 17, 2007.

[11] On Walter Markov's life and work see also: Neuhaus, Manfred/Seidel, Helmut/Diesener, Gerald/Middell, Matthias (eds.): *Wenn jemand seinen Kopf bewusst hinhielt... Beiträge zu Werk und Wirken von Walter Markov,* Rosa-Luxemburg-Stiftung Sachsen, Leipzig 1998^2. Markov, Walter: *Wie viele Leben lebt der Mensch. Eine Autobiographie aus dem Nachlaß*, Faber & Faber, Leipzig 2009.

Markov and Kossok had initiated a research programme on comparative revolutionary history in the 1970s that had repercussions far beyond the borders of the GDR.[12] In the 1960s, the circle consisting of Markov, Kossok and Katz (who were later joined by the Mexican historian Enrique Semo)[13] formed an important – if not the most important – network in the GDR for historiographical research and open discussions concerning Latin American issues.

1964 saw the publication of Katz' habilitation thesis, *Deutschland, Diaz und die Mexikanische Revolution. Die deutsche Politik in Mexico 1870–1920* (*Germany, Diaz and the Mexican Revolution. Germany's Mexican Policy 1870–1920*).[14] It exemplifies the third characteristic of Friedrich Katz' historiographical oeuvre: his pronounced preference for research involving primary sources and the historicist foundation of his work in the source-based reconstruction of the historical process. The habilition thesis had been supervised by Markov and openly displayed his influence. Markov had chosen as the subject of his own habilitation (approved in 1947) the history of German diplomacy in the Balkans and had used a research design associated with traditional diplomatic history – the study of files in the official archives of the Foreign Ministry and its predecessor institutions – to discuss questions that went far beyond what had been seen as its remit:[15] questions concerning the interplay of widely differing actors;

---

[12] For the comparative history of revolutions in Leipzig see also Middell, Matthias: *Weltgeschichtsschreibung im Zeitalter der Verfachlichung und Professionalisierung.* Vol. 3: *Von der vergleichenden Kulturgeschichte zur Revolutionskomparatistik*, Akademische Verlagsanstalt, Leipzig 2005. Mayer, David: Transnationale Debattengeflechte in marxistisch inspirierten Historiographien: Die Übergangsdebatten und ihre Rezeption in der DDR, in: Steidl, Annemarie et al. (eds.): *Übergänge und Schnittmengen. Arbeit, Migration, Bevölkerung und Wissenschaftsgeschichte in Diskussion*, Böhlau, Wien 2008, 284-289.

[13] Enrique Semo (b. 1930) pursued his doctoral studies at the Humboldt University between 1968 and 1971. His thesis, supervised by Manfred Kossok, *Die ökonomischen Ursprünge der mexikanischen Nation (1521–1759)*[*The Economic Origins of the Mexican Nation (1521–1759)*], dealt with the economic origins of the Mexican nation. For the close contacts between Semo, Katz and Kossok cf. the obituary for Friedrich Katz by Enrique Semo, in: http://mexicanstudies.uchicago.edu/page/essays#semo (retrieved on April 6, 2012).

[14] Katz, Friedrich: *Deutschland, Diaz und die mexikanische Revolution. Die deutsche Politik in Mexiko 1870–1920* (=Schriftenreihe des Instituts für Allgemeine Geschichte an der Humboldt-Universität Berlin 9), Deutscher Verlag d. Wissenschaften, Berlin 1964.

[15] Markov, Walter: *Grundzüge der Balkandiplomatie. Ein Beitrag zur Geschichte der Abhängigkeitsverhältnisse*, Leipziger Universitäts-Verlag, Leipzig 1999.

the "entanglement", as we would call it today, of historical processes playing out in different places; economic interdependences; and asymmetrical relationships and their symbolic-discursive underpinning. In his treatment of Germany's Mexican policy Katz proceeded along similar lines. It is this approach to diplomatic history, transcending as it did the discipline's traditional confines, that was to make him famous in the early 1980s when he came to write his enlarged study on great power policy towards Mexico during the Revolution. Therefore the secret behind *The Secret War*[16] is to be found not least in the East Berlin and/or Leipzig of the 1960s where a milieu devoted to a critical reflection of Marxism was developing in the lap of real Socialism.[17]

1968 became an important turning point for Katz – in his biography two venues of "global 1968" coincide:[18] Eastern Europe, facing, as we know today, the end of the hope that real Socialism might reconstitute itself; and Latin America, especially Mexico, where in the context of the "long 1960s" and inspired by the Cuban Revolution, pupils, students and small groups from other sectors of society were reviving for themselves the promises of freedom and social justice, the centrepieces of the unfinished agenda of the Mexican Revolution, until they were bloodily suppressed by the official custodian of that revolution, the PRI. Events in Eastern Europe and in the GDR had a sobering effect on Katz; he left the country with his family in 1970, a step that the privilege of their foreign passports enabled them to make. The Humboldt University had converted his post into a full professorship in September 1969, after only two years as an associate professor, which points to efforts being made by the University to persuade him to stay. After several guest professorships he found a new academic home in 1971 at the University of Chicago, a renowned and elite institution with a reputedly conservative tradition. In the Mexican context, Katz became part, after the Massacre at the *Plaza de las Tres Culturas*, of a development that resulted in the 1970s in a pluralization of voices at least in academic circles. New interpretations were being put forward in the historiography of the Mexican Revolution, all of them with highly charged political implications.

---

[16] Katz, Friedrich: *The Secret War in Mexico. Europe, the United States and the Mexican revolution*, University of Chicago Press, Chicago et al. 1981.

[17] A milieu, it must be said, that found itself repeatedly exposed to persecution and the exertion of pressure. Markov for instance was charged with Titoism in 1951 and expelled from the SED.

[18] Cf. Kastner, Jens/Mayer, David (eds.): *Weltwende 1968? Ein Jahr aus globalgeschichtlicher Perspektive*, Mandelbaum, Wien 2008.

This wave of new, "revisionist" interpretations of the Mexican Revolution, which began in the late 1960s and the early 1970s, included on the one hand studies focussed on sociohistorical aspects and, on the other, interpretations from a "bottom-up" perspective. Many of these studies openly declared their interest in reviving the Mexican Revolution, that is to say, in returning to its unfinished agenda. Authors like the US American John Womack, Adolfo Gilly, an activist from Argentina, and Arnaldo Córdova, a Mexican, started the ball rolling and many others followed.[19] Non-Mexican historians played an important role in this context. They included Friedrich Katz, who maintained a steady presence in Mexico with sociohistorical papers from the mid-1970s, until he presented *The Secret War* in the early 1980s, a work that was to find a broad readership and bring him the fame that accompanied him to the end of his life.

Katz was very mindful of the political implications of historiography, especially with regard to the history of revolutions. With the sweeping success of revisionist interpretations of the Mexican Revolution in the 1970s in mind,[20] Katz observed that the government "felt we had contributed to lending the Revolution a certain legitimacy both within the country and abroad. None of us of course asserted that the PRI was the upshot of the Revolution. But by calling [...] the Mexican Revolution a revolution, a categorisation rejected by the Conservatives, we were accepted automatically. This was what mattered most."[21] The different reinterpretations that have emerged since the 1970s have thus been driven by two contradictory forces: On the one hand, there was a far-reaching delegitimisation of the PRI government on the grounds of its non-fulfilment of revolutionary promises; on the other, there was a validation of that government's key claim in terms of the politics of history: that it owed its inception to a genuine revolution and not to prolonged senseless bloodshed.

---

[19] Womack Jr., John: *Zapata and the Mexican Revolution*, Knopf, New York 1969. Córdova, Arnaldo: *La ideología de la revolución mexicana. La formación del nuevo régimen*, ERA, México, D.F. 1973. Gilly, Adolfo: *La revolución interrumpida. México 1910–1920: una guerra campesina por la tierra y el poder*, El Caballito, México D.F. 1971.

[20] This revisionism was inspired to a large extent by Marxist interpretations, while the revisionist interpretations of the English or the French Revolution that were being put forward at about the same time were mostly critical of the preponderance of Marxist slants. For the many facets of revisionism in historiography cf. Traverso, Enzo: *Gebrauchsanleitungen für die Vergangenheit. Geschichte, Erinnerung, Politik,* Unrast, Münster 2007, 95-99.

[21] Interview with Friedrich Katz, Vienna, December 17, 2007 [my translation].

Katz however knew not only how much this meant to the Mexican state in terms of politics of history but also of the political and intellectual complexity of the Marxist categories that were used as guidelines in these new interpretations. In all this Katz maintained his own undoctrinaire and discreet Marxist stance. From overheated debates where adherents of different leftist trends were at each other's throats – a case in point is a volume on the Mexican Revolution consisting of papers written from Communist, Trotzkyist, Gramscian and Maoist standpoints[22] – Katz tellingly absented himself. Nor did he intervene in highly contentious debates in the 1970s on the respective roles played by "feudalism" and "capitalism" in the history of Latin America, at least not, as was fashionable at the time, in terms of theory or conceptual deduction. What did cause him to intervene were concrete sociohistorical questions. He was interested for instance in the nature of the prerevolutionary haziendas in Mexico and its bonded labour relationships (debt bondage, etc.), in the question, in short, whether the prerevolutionary hazienda had been a premodern agricultural institution, whose owner would have been motivated by considerations of "prestige", or whether it should be seen in the light of a capitalist enterprise, whose basis was the logic of the accumulation of capital.[23] The focus of Katz' publications in the 1970s was emphatically on issues of agrarian and social history.

Another almost ubiquitous Marxist debate of the 1970s that was notable for Katz' absence was the debate on modes of production in colonial Latin America. He explained his abstinence in an interview, saying, "I simply did not want to get involved; the whole thing seemed altogether too esoteric."[24] What did attract him was the controversy about the so-called Asiatic mode of production and the applicability of this concept to pre-Columbian societies. In Mexico this approach had found several important proponents such as Angel Palerm, Roger Bartra, Pedro Carrasco and Johanna Broda. Katz shared with these scholars a keen interest in Karl Wittfogel's classic *Oriental Despotism* and in Wittfogel's emphasis on the importance of irrigation infrastructure for premodern civiliza-

[22] Gilly, Adolfo/Córdova, Arnaldo/Bartra, Armando/Aguilar Mora, Manuel/Semo, Enrique: *Interpretaciones de la Revolución Mexicana*, Nueva Imagen, México, D.F. 1989[12] (1979).

[23] Katz, Friedrich: Condiciones de trabajo en las haciendas de México durante el porfiriato: modalidades y tendencias, in: Katz, Friedrich (ed.): *La servidumbre agraria en México en la época porfiriana* (=SepSetentas vol. 303), Secretaría de Educación Pública, México, D.F. 1976, 15-91. Katz, Friedrich: El campesinado en la revolución mexicana de 1910, in: *El Trimestre Económico* 1/4 (1976), 118-134.

[24] Interview with Friedrich Katz, Vienna December 17, 2007 [my translation].

tions (hydraulic societies).[25] Katz' interest in these discussions was motivated less by "American" than by "East European" considerations: while in Latin America the focus was on specific features of the Aztec, Maya and Inca civilizations, East European intellectuals, having rediscovered the "Asiatic mode of production" as a concept that had been suppressed under Stalin from the 1930s, were trying to apply it in their analysis of real Socialism. As the concept had been used by Marx for analysing societies without private ownership whose economy was controlled by an all-powerful state, it remained to be seen, in the eyes of those intellectuals, whether it could not be used for understanding real Socialism.[26] The underlying issue in this worldwide mesh of Marxist inspired debates was the same, though seen against different backgrounds and used with different motives – and Katz was one of only a handful of scholars who had a biographical and an intellectual rapport with both contexts.

Katz also integrated the second great trend of Marxist inspired historical analysis into his work: the interest in agency, especially the agency of the majority of the population, which is not usually discernible in the classic "archive". The capacity of becoming active, of intervening, was of great interest for Katz both in the case of collectives, as is evident from his above-mentioned works on agrarian movements, and of individuals; evidence for the latter is his last great work, where he deals with the legendary leader of the Mexican Revolution in the country's north, Francisco "Pancho" Villa.[27] It is by virtue of his Marxist inspired interest in socially embedded agency that Katz manages, in *The Life and Times of Pancho Villa*, to avoid the pitfalls inherent in the biographical genre – inappropriate psychologizing, hyper individualization, teleological speculations on "biographical patterns", kitschy hero worship – and present a critical portrait of the near mythical, multifaceted actor in all his ambivalence. At the same time Katz fully avails himself of the advantages of the biographical genre – the rich palette of narrative reconstruction, which is not confined to mere analysis, the attention to detail and a certain empathy for his (anti-)hero. It is the life *and* the

---

[25] Wittfogel, Karl August: *Oriental Despotism. A Comparative Study of Total Power*, Yale University Press, New Haven 1957. Wittfogel, Karl August: *The Hydraulic Civilizations*, University of Chicago Press, Chicago 1956.

[26] On the twists and turns of the discussion on the Asiatic mode of production cf. O'Leary, Brendan: *The Asiatic Mode of Production. Oriental Despotism, Historical Materialism and Indian History* (with a foreword by Ernest Gellner), Basil Blackwell, Oxford et al. 1989.

[27] Katz, Friedrich: *The Life and Times of Pancho Villa*, Stanford University Press, Stanford 1998.

times of Pancho Villa, it is analysis *and* narrative and it is the inspiration that Marxist categories can provide – without, at the same time, imposing themselves on the text – that this late work manages to incorporate.

The works of Friedrich Katz combine many and widely differing historiographical methods and styles; the same cannot be said of many twentieth century historians. Another strong point in his suit as a historian is his tone: compared to the hubub of the debates on the Mexican Revolution in the early 1970s, with their alarmist immediacy and pressing urgency – the activists of the time, listening to their own quickening heartbeat, clearly felt that a revival of the revolution was imminent – Katz' writings, while by no means devoid of empathy and passion, signal calmness and circumspection. His message seemed to be, sure enough, it has been a revolution, but that is no reason to go crazy. The virtue of keeping things in proportion, old-fashioned but fundamental for any proponent of historiography, found a consummate partisan in Friedrich Katz.

Die Selbstermächtigung der Maus. Friedrich Katz und das Überleben

Berthold Molden

Zeit seines Lebens war Friedrich Katz an verschiedenen Orten verwurzelt, ob diese nun geographischer oder epistemologischer, kultureller oder politischer Natur waren. Über seine Rolle in der Historiographiegeschichte und seine Verbindungen zur mexikanischen Geschichte im Besonderen ist viel gesagt und geschrieben worden, unter anderem auch in diesem Band. Auf den folgenden Seiten stelle ich eine Assoziationskette um einen Aspekt von Leben und Werk des großen Historikers vor, der mir bedeutend scheint für ein vollständiges Verständnis von Friedrich Katz: seine Identität (obwohl er diesen Begriff wohl nur mit gewisser ironischer Skepsis gebraucht hätte) als Überlebender. Ich werde mir einige Volten erlauben, die auf den ersten Blick als argumentative Sprünge oder gewagte Assoziationen erscheinen mögen, jedoch zu einem justierten Blick auf Katz beitragen sollen.

Am 8. August 1942 schrieb der Vertreter des Jüdischen Weltkongresses in Genf, Gerhard Riegner, ein Telegramm, in dem er jene Information über die von den Nationalsozialisten so genannte „Endlösung" zusammenfasste, welche ihm ein deutscher Informant überbracht hatte. Riegners Schreiben richtete sich an seinen Präsidenten in New York, Rabbi Stephen Wise. Die Nazis, schrieb er, wollten vier Millionen Juden deportieren, konzentrieren und vernichten. In der Geschichtsschreibung gilt dieses „Riegner-Telegramm" als Schlüsselbeleg für den Holocaust in einer Welt und Zeit, die – aus unterschiedlichen Gründen – die volle Dimension der NS-Verbrechen nicht glauben wollte. Sein Inhalt, darunter Information über Vernichtungslager und den Einsatz von Cyanwasserstoff, wurde ab November 1942 verschiedentlich veröffentlicht. Dennoch, und trotz des Einsatzes jüdischer Organisationen in den USA, nahmen weder die amerikanische noch die internationale Presse diese Nachricht besonders ernst.

Kaum ein halbes Jahr nach der Publikation des Riegner-Telegramms wurde in Mexiko-Stadt ein Band herausgegeben, der mittlerweile als eine der ersten Wahrnehmungen der Shoa in der Welt und vor allem außerhalb Europas und der USA eingeschätzt wird, unter anderem mit der Illustration *Deportación a la muerte* (*Deportation in den Tod*) von Leopoldo Méndez.[1] Dabei handelt es sich

[1] Merfish, Beth: El Libro Negro. Mexico City at the Front of Antifascism, in: *ArtUS* 1 (2009), 36-41, hier 37.

um das *Libro negro del terror nazi en Europa* (*Schwarzbuch des Nazi-Terrors in Europa*), eines von insgesamt sechs spanischsprachigen Büchern, die der berühmte Exilverlag der linken Exilanten in Mexiko, El Libro Libre, herausbrachte.[2] Mit seinen 10.000 Exemplaren brachte es der Band auf über die Hälfte der gesamten spanischsprachigen Druckauflage des Verlages. Die übrigen 20 Bücher, die zwischen 1942 und 1946 dort verlegt wurden, waren Werke in deutscher Sprache aus der Feder von so prominenten linken Autorinnen und Autoren wie Anna Seghers, Lion Feuchtwanger, Egon Erwin Kisch, Heinrich Mann, Paul Merker oder – Leo Katz.

Das *Libro negro del terror nazi en Europa* richtete sich an die spanischsprachige Welt. Dieses Publikum war eben erst in einen Krieg eingetreten, der in gewisser Weise entrückt blieb – trotz der zahlreichen europäischen Flüchtlinge mit ihrer Brücken- und Informationsfunktion zwischen dem brennenden Europa und Mexiko. Der Historiker und Romancier Paco Ignacio Taibo II beschrieb diese Situation für das Jahr 1941 wie folgt: „Ganz sicher wird zuviel gestorben, aber Europa ist weit weg. Es herrscht Krieg. Zu uns dringt nur ein Echo. Echos haben keine Schneide, lassen kein Blut fließen."[3] Die Gemeinschaft der Vertriebenen, die in Mexiko-Stadt zusammengekommen war, fungierte als Quelle ebenso wie als Verstärker dieses transatlantischen Echos. Taibo II schildert die Enttäuschung von Seghers, Kisch und anderen über die Regierung von Ávila Camacho und ihre neue Haltung, den Nationalismus über den Sozialismus (und damit die internationale Solidarität) zu stellen, was eine restriktivere Asyl- und Immigrationspolitik bedeutete.[4] Der Widerhall der Weltpolitik war nicht nur in Diskursen von Regierung und Presse, sondern auch in Exilantenkreisen zu vernehmen. In einer ersten intergenerationellen Assoziation – also Vater und Sohn Katz – wird Friedrich Katz' Geschichtsschreibung zur Verstärkung des Echos der Mexikanischen Revolution. In leidenschaftlicher Auseinandersetzung mit der historischen Emergenz jenes Landes, das ihm das Leben gerettet und diese erste Anklage Entkommener gegen die Shoa ermöglicht hatte, verortete Katz die Revolution nicht allein in einer transnationalen Analyse, sondern kreierte selbst ein neues internationales Interesse durch seine wegweisenden Werke.

---

[2] Meyer, Hannes (Hg.): *El Libro negro del terror nazi en Europa*, El Libro Libre, México, D.F. 1943.

[3] Taibo II, Paco Ignacio: *Die Rückkehr der Schatten*, Assoziation A, Berlin/Hamburg/Göttingen 2005, 25.

[4] Hier gestatte ich mir freilich, einen komplexen historischen Prozess auf eine einfache Formel zu reduzieren.

Es war also in Mexiko, dem Land, wo der „abweichlerische Jude“ Trotzki zuerst Asyl und dann den Tod von Hand des stalinistischen Agenten Ramón Mercader fand; im einzigen Land der Welt, das im März 1938 gegen den so genannten Anschluss Österreichs an Deutschland protestierte; in Mexiko war es, wo ein kommunistischer Verlag die Verfolgung und Vernichtung des europäischen Judentums in sein kollektives „J'accuse!“ gegen den Nationalsozialismus aufnahm. Dies stellt eine tragende Säule im schütteren Pantheon marxistischer Holocaustdeutungen während des Krieges und in den ersten Nachkriegsdekaden dar. So erschien der Band etwa ein Jahr vor Adornos und Horkheimers berühmter *Dialektik der Aufklärung*, die 1944 ebenfalls im transatlantischen Exil in New York publiziert wurde. Nach der unmittelbaren Nachkriegszeit dauerte es dann, wie der Historiker Enzo Traverso bemerkte, bis in die 1980er Jahre, ehe das Thema vom Marxisten Ernest Mandel tiefgehend analysiert wurde – in Fortführung von Trotzkis Gedanken zur „Judenfrage“.[5]

In Mexiko-Stadt schrieb Leo Katz auch für jiddische Zeitungen und bewegte sich damit in unterschiedlichen Exilantenmilieus, wodurch Friedrich in einem höchst heterogenen sozialen Umfeld aufwuchs. Seine damaligen Freunde Enrique Semo[6] und Rodolfo Stavenhagen[7] geben von der Vielfalt dieser Welt Zeugnis ab. Doch im Jahre 1949 kehrte der Kommunist Leo Katz nach Wien zurück, um seine politische Arbeit als Autor und Journalist wieder aufzunehmen. Als er Mexiko nach einem Jahrzehnt des Exils und politischen Engagements verließ, folgte ihm seine Familie nach Wien. Für den damals 22jährigen Friedrich Katz bedeutete dies die Rückkehr in eine unbekannte Heimat, war er doch schon im Alter von drei Jahren nach Berlin übersiedelt. 1949 hatte Katz das Wagner College in New York und eine postgraduelle Ausbildung an der mexikanischen Escuela Nacional de Antropología e Historia absolviert. In Wien

---

[5] Traverso, Enzo: Von der Frankfurter Schule zu Ernest Mandel. Fragestellungen und Sackgassen des Marxismus hinsichtlich Auschwitz, in: Traverso, Enzo: *Nach Auschwitz. Die Linke und die Aufarbeitung des NS-Völkermordes*, ISP Verlag, Köln 2000, 79-104, hier 82.

[6] Zu Enrique Semo vgl. Fußnote 13 in David Mayers Beitrag zu diesem Band *Der Weltenläufer: Friedrich Katz und die historiographischen Debatten seiner Zeit*.

[7] Rodolfo Stavenhagen (geb. 1932) ist ein mexikanischer Soziologe am Colegio de México. Unter anderem war er stellvertretender Generaldirektor der UNESCO und bis 2008 der erste „UN-Sonderberichterstatter zur Lage der Menschenrechte und Grundlegenden Freiheiten Indigener Völker“.

arbeitete er wie sein Vater für die kommunistische Tageszeitung *Volksstimme*,[8] vor allem aber setzte er seine Studien der mesoamerikanischen Geschichte fort und promovierte 1954 mit einer Arbeit über die ökonomische Struktur der vorkolumbischen Azteken.

Nun wollen wir kurz in jenem Moment innehalten, da Friedrich Katz seine erste Arbeit über die Mexikanische Revolution veröffentlichte. Er tat dies in Ost-Berlin. Katz begab sich 1956 in die Deutsche Demokratische Republik, als die Entstalinisierung in der Sowjetunion eben zur offiziellen Staatspolitik wurde, nicht jedoch in allen Teilen Zentral- und Osteuropas. Gerade die DDR-Führung blieb in dieser Hinsicht besonders reformfeindlich. Nur vier Jahre zuvor hatte das Mitglied des Zentralkomitees der SED Alexander Abusch, der selbst als Exilant in Mexiko gewesen war, Leo Katz und andere als Vertreter einer „jüdisch-chauvinistischen Linie“ denunziert.[9] In stalinistischer Weltsicht implizierte die Thematisierung des Holocaust und der historischen Verantwortung Deutschlands, wenn dieser auch eine wichtige politisch-propagandistische Funktion zukam, oft einen antizionistischen Ton. Abusch selbst musste 1950 aufgrund des „Falls Merker“ seine Ämter eine Zeit lang zurücklegen und auch 1956 hatte Chruschtschows rezente Abrechnung mit Stalin vor dem XX. Parteitag der KPdSU das Ambiente jedenfalls in der DDR noch nicht verändert. Dennoch übersiedelte Katz nach Berlin, um bis Ende der 1960er Jahre an der Humboldt-Universität zu arbeiten. Dort wurde er 1962 mit einer Arbeit habilitiert, die sich bereits mit der Mexikanischen Revolution beschäftigte und 1964 unter dem Titel *Deutschland, Diaz und die mexikanische Revolution* erschien.[10] In diesem Werk und anderen zeitnahen Publikationen[11] reihte sich Katz unter die Ersten, die sich ausführlich mit einem anderen „deutschen Telegramm“ von enormer Tragweite beschäftigten: jenem des deutschen Außenministers Arthur Zimmermann vom 19. Januar 1917, das sich für den Fall eines Eintritts der USA in den Ersten Weltkrieg um eine Allianz mit Mexiko bemühte und diesem dafür Texas, New Mexico und Arizona in Aussicht stellte. Eine Nachricht im Übrigen, die viel

---

[8] Leo Katz schrieb für die *Volksstimme* bis zu seinem Tod im Jahre 1954 – 14 Monate, ehe die Rote Armee aus Österreich abrückte und der Stalinplatz wieder in Schwarzenbergplatz umbenannt wurde.

[9] Herf, Jeffrey: *Divided Memory: The Nazi Past in Two Germanys*, Harvard University Press, Cambridge 1997, 135.

[10] Katz, Friedrich: *Deutschland, Diaz und die mexikanische Revolution: Die deutsche Politik in Mexiko 1870–1920* (=Schriftenreihe des Instituts für Allgemeine Geschichte an der Humboldt-Universität Berlin 9), Deutscher Verlag d. Wissenschaften, Berlin 1964.

[11] Katz, Friedrich: Alemania y Francisco Villa, in: *Historia Mexicana* 12 (1962), 88-102.

stärkeren Einfluss auf die US-Politik ihrer Zeit hatte als ein Vierteljahrhundert später das eingangs erwähnte Telegramm Gerhard Riegners, gilt es doch mit als auslösender Faktor für Woodrow Wilsons Entscheidung zur Kriegserklärung.

Man erkennt hier, wie sich Katz' unermüdliches Interesse an internationaler Geschichte und diachronen wie synchronen globalen Vergleichen auf die Mexikanische Revolution richtet. Deutschland als zentraler Akteur während der Revolutionsperiode betrat die internationale Bühne, welche bislang vor allem vom mächtigen nördlichen Nachbarn, den USA, sowie Großbritannien und Frankreich dominiert worden war. Doch Katz beschränkte sich nicht auf Variationen der Kriegsschuldfrage, die seit 1945 wieder verstärkt diskutiert wurde, um ein historisches Muster in den Katastrophen der letzten Jahrzehnte zu finden. Er ging darüber hinaus. 1966 gab er einen Band über den deutschen Faschismus in Lateinamerika mit heraus, der 1968 auch in Mexiko veröffentlicht wurde.[12] In gleichsam gespiegelter Weise folgte er den Schritten seines Vaters, der mitten im Krieg die Geschichten bekannter Antifaschisten eingesetzt hatte, um die Verbrechen eines infernalischen Regimes anzuklagen. Der Sohn, nun zum Historiker geworden, wollte zu den wissenschaftlichen Bemühungen seiner Zeit beitragen, den „Internationalismus" der Nazis über Quellen zu verstehen, die mittlerweile Geschichte waren.

Es mutet fast wie ein dialektischer Zufall an, dass exakt 30 Jahre später ein anderer zeitweise in Mexiko Exilierter, der zu diesem Zeitpunkt bereits in einem anderen Land lebte, sozusagen den Spieß nochmals umdrehte. In dem Roman *Die Naziliteratur in Amerika* schuf der chilenische, von seiner Zeit in Mexiko nachhaltig geprägte Schriftsteller Roberto Bolaño ein fiktives Universum nazistischer Literatur, um seinerseits zeitgenössische totalitäre Tendenzen in Lateinamerika anzugreifen.[13] Der Bolaño von 1996, so formulierte ein Kritiker, „erfindet die Geschichte aus der Referenzialität der Ereignisse".[14] Der Friedrich Katz von 1966 referenzierte die Ereignisse zu ihrer globalhistorischen Bedeutung. Beide fanden in Schlüsselmomenten ihrer Jugend in Mexiko Zuflucht vor Diktatur und Tod.[15] Beide wandten sich immer und immer

---

[12] Katz, Friedrich/Sanke, Heinz (Hg.): *Der Deutsche Faschismus in Lateinamerika 1933–1943*, Humboldt-Universität zu Berlin, Berlin 1966. Katz, Friedrich (Hg.): *Hitler sobre América Latina: el fascismo alemán en Latinoamérica 1933–1943. 4 investigaciones históricas*, Fondo de Cultura Popular, México, D.F. 1968.

[13] Bolaño, Roberto: *Die Naziliteratur in Amerika*, Kunstmann, München 1999. Bolaño, Roberto: *La literatura nazi en las Américas*, Seix Barral, Barcelona 1996.

[14] Peiró, José Vincente: ¿Quién puede comprender mi terror mejor que usted?, in: *Turia* 75/9 (2005), 211-214, hier 212 [Übersetzung B. M.].

[15] Hiermit ist freilich keinerlei struktureller Vergleich zwischen dem Nationalsozialismus und dem Pinochet-Regime intendiert.

wieder jenen gesellschaftlich-politischen Konstellationen zu, welche die transnationale Signifikanz dieses Mexikos ausmachten. Sie begeisterten sich für verschiedene Protagonisten der Revolution und sie teilten, wenn auch aus höchst unterschiedlichen Perspektiven, die Faszination für das US-mexikanische Grenzgebiet.

Weshalb aber widmen wir uns dieser besonderen Etappe in Leben und Werk des Historikers Friedrich Katz? Und worin besteht die in meinen Augen tiefere Verbindung mit Bolaño? Darauf gibt es mehrere Detailantworten. So lässt sich an dieser Periode erstmals die transnationale Analyse historischer Zusammenhänge beobachten, die zu Katz' Markenzeichen werden sollte – ohne dass er darüber mikrohistorische Präzision in seinen Quellenstudien vernachlässigt hätte. Und man kann, mit Bolaños fiktiven Büchern und Autoren vor Augen, an jene Episode denken, als Leo Katz die Subskribentenliste der deutschen *Nationalzeitung* in Mexiko in die Hände bekam und dem NS-freundlichen deutschen Publikum eine komplette Ausgabe mit fingierten Nachrichten ins Haus schickte. Doch über diese Details hinaus verweist diese Assoziation zwischen zwei Intellektuellen, die einander wohl nicht kannten, auf Wichtigeres.

Im letzten Interview mit Bolaño kurz vor seinem Tod 2003 wurde dem Schriftsteller die Frage gestellt: „Sind Sie Chilene, Spanier oder Mexikaner?" Er antwortete: „Ich bin Lateinamerikaner."[16] Im April 2000 hatte Roberto Bolaño Wien besucht, wo seit zwei Monaten die umstrittene Koalition des Christdemokraten Wolfgang Schüssel mit der rechtsextremen FPÖ regierte. Er kam, um an dem Seminar „Europa – Lateinamerika: Literatur, Migration und Identität" teilzunehmen, las im Instituto Cervantes aus dem Roman *La literatura nazi* und wurde zum Abendessen in die mexikanische Botschaft eingeladen, „wo die sympathische Botschafterin [...] mich wie einen Mexikaner behandelte".[17] Und er hielt seine bekannte *Wiener Rede* mit dem Titel *Literatur und Exil* (er sprach im Zusammenhang mit dem Exil immer von Vertreibung, als wolle er keine verharmlosende Vorstellung von freiwilliger Auswanderung aufkommen lassen), in der er erklärte, „meine Heimat sind mein Sohn und meine Bibliothek", denn „ein Arbeiter soll nicht nostalgisch sein: Seine Hände sind seine Heimat."[18]

---

[16] Bolaño, Roberto: Estrella distante (entrevista de Mónica Maristain), in: Bolaño, Roberto: *Entre paréntesis. Ensayos, artículos y discursos (1998–2003)* (herausgegeben von Ignacio Echevarría), Anagrama, Barcelona 2004, 329-343, hier 331 [Übersetzung B. M.].

[17] Roberto Bolaño, Viena y la sombra de una mujer, in: Bolaño, Roberto: *Entre paréntesis. Ensayos, artículos y discursos (1998–2003)* (herausgegeben von Ignacio Echevarría), Anagrama, Barcelona 2004, 250-253, hier 253 [Übersetzung B. M.].

[18] Roberto Bolaño, Literatura y exilio, in: Bolaño, Roberto: *Entre paréntesis. Ensayos, artículos y discursos (1998–2003)* (herausgegeben von Ignacio Echevarría), Anagrama, Barcelona 2004, 40-46, hier 43 [Übersetzung B. M.].

Auch über Friedrich Katz gibt es ein Essay, das sich der Historizität seines Lebens über fiktive Parallelbiographien anzunähern versucht. In diesem Text erwähnt sein Autor, der Historiker Mauricio Tenorio, eine akademische Begegnung, in der eine

> „affige Historikerin [Katz] in die Enge trieb, die Frage zu beantworten: ‚Und du, Friedrich, als was fühlst du dich eher: Mexikaner, Deutscher oder US-Amerikaner?' Professor Katz beschränkte sich darauf zu korrigieren, dass er niemals Deutscher gewesen, dass er Österreicher sei und dass er Mexiko bewundere, das Land, das ihn und seine Familie gerettet hatte, aber: ‚Wenn ich denn diese Frage beantworten muss, würde ich sagen, ich bin Überlebender, ich bin einer von denen, die sich retten konnten'."[19]

Katz als Überlebender? Diese Selbstbeschreibung mag überraschen. Gewiss, Enrique Semo erinnerte sich während der Festschriftpräsentation für Friedrich Katz an der Columbia University im November 2010, dass Katz und er „derselben Generation von Überlebenden" angehörten. Bei derselben Veranstaltung erwähnte Adolfo Gilly eben jenen oben zitierten Absatz Tenorios und fügte hinzu, Katz' Worte seien „von ganzem Herzen gekommen". Doch er erklärte auch, dass „der Sinn, den [Katz] in seiner eigenen Geschichte fand", eine offene Frage bleibe.[20]

Wie dem auch sei, das Überleben ist eine Kategorie, die wichtig ist für das Verständnis des großen Forschers und Lehrers, der in eindrucksvoller Weise die Geschichtsschreibung über mehrere Epochen und Regionen Lateinamerikas beeinflusste. Obwohl sein an Übersiedlungen reiches Leben ursprünglich durch die Flucht vor dem Faschismus einen ersten Impuls erhalten hatte und trotz seiner doppelten Betroffenheit durch den Nazi-Terror (eine kommunistische Familie jüdischer Abstammung), wird er kaum als Überlebender identifiziert. Vielleicht liegt es daran, dass dieser Begriff oft mit dem des Opfers zusammenfällt und daher jeder Handlungsmacht entkleidet scheint. Gerade das Beispiel Friedrich Katz zeigt jedoch, dass diese Verbindung nicht zwingend ist.

Art Spiegelman nannte seinen berühmten Comic, der vom Überleben seines Vaters zur Zeit des Holocaust und danach erzählt, *Maus. A Survivor's Tale*. Viele Literaturwissenschaftler haben sich um eine Interpretation dieses Titels

---

[19] Tenorio Trillo, Mauricio: Vidas Imaginarias, in: Garciadiego, Javier/Kourí, Emilio (Hg.): *Revolución y exilio en la historia de México. Del amor de un historiador a su patria adoptiva: Homenaje a Friedrich Katz*, ERA/University of Chicago/El Colegio de México, México, D.F./Chicago 2010, 89-104, hier 90 [Übersetzung B. M.].

[20] Zit. nach den Videoaufzeichnungen dieser Veranstaltung in: http://www.youtube.com/watch?v=ktrHM03lp88 (Zugriff 22. Mai 2012) [Übersetzung B. M.].

bemüht, doch immerhin scheint ein Konsens darüber zu bestehen, dass die Maus der Katze als unendlich stärkerer und demnach tödlicher Spezies gegenübersteht. So sind bei Spiegelman die Katzen die deutschen Nazis, die zur Vernichtung der „jüdischen Mäuse“ ansetzen. Doch Spiegelman war nicht der Erste, der die Maus ermächtigte und mit einer Handlungskraft ausstattete, die sehr wohl auf die Veränderbarkeit der Welt vertraute, selbst gegen die schlimmsten Widrigkeiten: Leo Katz hatte das Pseudonym „Maus“ bereits als Journalist im Berlin der Weimarer Republik verwendet. Auch wenn die Etymologie des Namens Katz nichts mit Katzen zu tun hat, sondern eine Form von Kohn oder Cohen ist, wirkt die Analogie. Die aktivistische Maus überlebt die Apokalypse der Katzen und bewahrt in Folge nicht nur ihr Interesse an den sozialen Strukturen der Welt, sondern auch einen „tiefen historischen Optimismus“.[21] Friedrich Katz hat beide Eigenschaften mit seinem Vater gemeinsam, ja mehr noch, beide verwandelten sich in maßgebliche Elemente seiner Arbeit als Historiker.

Claudio Lomnitz rekapitulierte im Zuge des erwähnten Festaktes der Columbia University die Katz'sche Perspektive auf die mexikanische Geschichte unter diesem Aspekt:

> „Mexico's twentieth century was shaped by exile. Friedrich is probably the person who has seen this most clearly first and foremost. First, the exile of Mexicans [...] and then Mexico as a place that received exiles, exiles who contributed to shaping Mexico in the imagination. Friedrich was one of these exiles, and he had the peculiarity of writing a history of Mexico that de-centered the national narrative as only an exile can do. Showing consistently similarities between Mexico and other places in the world, looking for international connections and demonstrating their significance even for the keystone event of Mexico's modern history, which is its social revolution at the beginning of the twentieth century.“

Lomnitz fuhr mit der Beobachtung fort, dass sich das Werk des Friedrich Katz gerade dadurch von anderen Diplomatiegeschichten unterscheide, dass der Autor über keine privilegierte Perspektive verfüge, weder eine mexikanische, noch eine deutsche oder amerikanische. Die Geschichte internationaler Beziehungen und die Regionalgeschichte der Grenzregion seien „synthesized in Friedrich's work, bringing together diplomatic, social and political history in a way that

---

[21] Kloyber, Christian: México/Datos biográficos, in: Douer, Alisa/Seeber, Ursula (Hg.): *Qué lejos está Viena. Latinoamérica como lugar de exilio de escritores y artistas austríacos*, Forschungs- und Dokumentationsstelle für Neuere Österreichische Literatur, Wien 1995, 112 [Übersetzung B. M.].

only an exile could hope to accomplish. There is no privileged identification."[22] Katz schrieb über Mexiko aus einer, wenn auch herzenswarmen Distanz, nicht allein weil sich sein Schreibtisch gerade in Österreich, Deutschland oder den USA befand. Vielmehr verdankte sich dieser Anteil nehmende Abstand einem authentischen, auf historischer Kritik beruhenden Kosmopolitismus. In diesem Sinne verglich ihn Lomnitz mit dem globalgeschichtlichen Blick, den andere vertriebene Österreicher seines Kalibers wie Eric Wolf und Eric Hobsbawm entwickelten.

Doch wie kann das Ausmaß benannt werden, in dem Katz' Leben sich in seiner Art der historischen Analyse niederschlug? Nochmals sei Claudio Lomnitz zitiert, der über die Familie Katz schrieb:

> „They were protected by the Mexican consul in Marseille – Gilberto Bosques – and brought to Mexico as political exiles. In other words, Katz' defence of the Mexican Revolution was also personal, and this made him beloved as a Mexican. [...] But Katz also belonged to an academic generation [...] in which he represented minority concerns – sometimes as a Jew, sometimes as a Communist, sometimes as a European who thought that Mexico and its Revolution had something to teach the world."[23]

Es waren Friedrich Katz und Christian Kloyber, die im Juni 2003 bei der Gemeinde Wien die Benennung eines Weges an der Donau nach Gilberto Bosques erwirkten. Eine positive Intervention in die nicht immer unproblematische Geschichtspolitik der Stadt im öffentlichen Raum. Und eine Möglichkeit für Katz, seine große Dankbarkeit gegenüber dem mexikanischen Diplomaten zu bekunden, der tausende Leben wie das der Familie Katz gerettet hatte.

Am Ende seines großen Buches über Pancho Villa und seine Zeit erzählt Friedrich Katz eine Anekdote über Villa, der 1935 in Form eines Hollywoodfilms zu einer wichtigen Referenz für junge österreichische Sozialisten im Kampf gegen die austrofaschistische Diktatur wurde. Er schloss, dass in der Mitte des 19. Jahrhunderts „an Austrian, Maximilian of Habsburg, had gone to Mexico to set up an authoritarian empire. Now, in one of history's ironies, the image of a Mexican revolutionary, in the shape of Pancho Villa, had come to Austria and became an instrument of democratic struggle in that country."[24]

---

[22] Zit. nach den Videoaufzeichnungen dieser Veranstaltung in: http://www.youtube.com/watch?v=ktrHM03lp88 (Zugriff 22. Mai 2012).

[23] Lomnitz, Claudio: On the Improbable Popularity of Friedrich Katz, in: *Estudios Mexicanos* 27/1 (2011), 233-239, hier 237 und 239.

[24] Katz, Friedrich: *The Life and Times of Pancho Villa*, Stanford University Press, Stanford 1998, 818.

In einer weiteren historischen Volte verhalf Friedrich Katz jenem Retter Unzähliger, dem Konsul Bosques, zu einer späten Ehrung in seiner Geburtsstadt, wo er selbst nach seiner Rückkehr 1949 den Nachkriegsantisemitismus gegenüber den Überlebenden erfahren musste. (Und wo, wenn auch unter viel weniger existenziellen Umständen, eine andere gastfreundliche Diplomatin Roberto Bolaño zum Mexikaner machte.) Wenige Wochen nach der Beisetzung von Friedrich Katz in der neuen jüdischen Sektion des Wiener Zentralfriedhofs sagte Adolfo Gilly über seinen verstorbenen Freund: „The one who survived is now back in Vienna.“[25] Gerade hier also, vielleicht mehr noch als anderswo, sind wir gut beraten, den vielen Wendungen in seinem Leben und Überleben auf den Grund zu gehen.

[25] Zit. nach den Videoaufzeichnungen dieser Veranstaltung in: http://www.youtube.com/watch?v=ktrHM03lp88 (Zugriff 22. Mai 2012).

The Self-Empowerment of the Mouse. The life and survival of Friedrich Katz

Berthold Molden

Throughout his life, Friedrich Katz cast anchor in waters of many different kinds: geographical, epistemological, cultural and political. Much has already been said and written, not least in this volume, about his role as a historiographer and the many ties that link him especially to the history of Mexico. In the following pages I will be presenting a chain of associations, focussing on one particular aspect of the great historian's life and work that seems indispensable to me if we are to understand Friedrich Katz more fully: his identity – a term, admittedly, that he himself would invariably have used with a generous pinch of ironical scepticism – as a survivor. In my attempts to outline this aspect I will allow myself a couple of volte-faces, which may at first look like insufficiently argued leaps or far-fetched associations but will be found, I trust, to contribute to a more clear-sighted appreciation of Friedrich Katz.

On August 8, 1942, the Geneva representative of the World Jewish Congress, Gerhard Riegner, dispatched a telegram in which he summed up the information on what the Nazis called the "Final Solution" that had been passed on to him by a German informant. Riegner told the president of his organisation in New York, Rabbi Stephen Wise, that the Nazis wanted to round up four million Jews, put them in concentration camps and exterminate them. Historians consider Riegner's telegram crucial evidence that the world had learned about the Holocaust at a time when people were not yet prepared for various reasons to see the Nazi crimes for what they were. Its contents, including information on the extermination camps and the use of hydrogen cyanide, were repeatedly published from November 1942 onwards. The efforts of Jewish organisations in the USA notwithstanding, this provoked little reaction and neither the US nor the international press took much notice of the matter.

Less than half a year after the publication of Riegner's telegram a book was published in Mexico City, which is currently considered to be one of the first indications that the Holocaust was gaining recognition even in countries outside Europe and the United States; among the things it contains is Leopoldo Méndez's graphic *Deportación a la muerte* (*Deportation to Death*).[1] That book was

[1] Merfish, Beth: El Libro Negro. Mexico City at the Front of Antifascism, in: *ArtUS* 1 (2009), 36-41, here 37.

the *Libro negro del terror nazi en Europa* (*The Black Book of Nazi Terror in Europe*), one of six books in Spanish published by El Libro Libre, the famous publishing house of leftist exiles in Mexico.[2] With its print run of 10,000 copies the book represented more than half the volume of the publisher's output in Spanish. Twenty books published by El Libro Libre between 1942 and 1946 were written in German by such well-known leftist authors as Anna Seghers, Lion Feuchtwanger, Egon Erwin Kisch, Heinrich Mann, Paul Merker and – Leo Katz.

The *Libro negro del terror nazi en Europa* was written for a Spanish-speaking readership, which had only just begun to become aware of the war. In view of the numerous refugees from Europe whom one would have expected to serve as so many bridges to the conflagration engulfing Europe and as so many channels of information, this may seem surprising but it was nevertheless a fact. The historian and novelist Paco Ignacio Taibo II described the situation in 1941 as follows: "Certainly too many people are dying, but Europe is so far away. There is a war going on. We live in its echoes. Echoes have no edges; they draw no blood."[3] The community of refugees that had gathered in Mexico City functioned as a source of the transatlantic echo and as its amplifier. Taibo II also describes how keenly disappointed Seghers, Kisch and others were with the government of Ávila Camacho and his decision to place nationalism above socialism (and international solidarity), paving the way to a more restrictive asylum and immigration policy.[4] The repercussions of global political developments were felt not only in the discourses of the government and the press, but also among the exiles. In a first intergenerational association involving Katz father and son, Friedrich Katz' achievements as a historian amount to an amplification of the echo generated by the Mexican Revolution. In his impassioned account of the historical emergence of the country that had saved his life and made that first indictment of the Holocaust possible by someone who had escaped from it, Katz not only assigns that revolution its place in a transnational analysis but creates new international interest in it through his seminal works.

---

[2] Meyer, Hannes (ed.): *El Libro negro del terror nazi en Europa*, El Libro Libre, México, D.F. 1943.

[3] Taibo II, Paco Ignacio: *Returning as Shadows*, Thomas Dunne Books, New York 2003, 19-20.

[4] This is of course the reduction of a complex historical development to a simplistic formula for the sake of brevity.

All this happened in Mexico, the country in which the "dissenting Jew" Trotsky had first found refuge and then death at the hand of Stalin's agent Ramón Mercader; which had been the only country in the entire world to lodge a protest in March 1938 against Austria's so-called *Anschluss*, the country's annexation by, and integration into, Germany; and it was in Mexico that a communist publishing house subsumed the persecution and destruction of European Jewry under its collective "J'accuse!" and thrust it into Hitler Germany's face. This, when all is said and done, was one of the few arrows from the not overly productive quiver of Marxist Holocaust interpretation during the war and in the first post-war decades. The book appeared roughly one year before Adorno's and Horkheimer's famous *Dialectic of Enlightenment*, published in 1944 also in transatlantic exile in New York. Many years elapsed after the end of the war before this theme, as the historian Enzo Traverso has noted, was taken up and analysed in the 1980s by the Marxist Ernest Mandel – in an elaboration of Trotsky's thoughts on the "Jewish question".[5]

In Mexico City Leo Katz also wrote for Yiddish newspapers and moved in émigré circles that could hardly have been more diverse, thus giving Friedrich the chance to grow up in an extremely heterogeneous social environment. His circle of friends at the time, which included Enrique Semo[6] and Rodolfo Stavenhagen[7], illustrates the multifaceted quality of this world. In 1949 however, the Communist Leo Katz returned to Vienna to resume his political work as author and journalist. When he left Mexico at the end of a decade of political activity in exile, his family followed him to Vienna. For Friedrich Katz, who was 22 at the time, this meant a return to an unknown native country that he had left for Berlin at the age of three. By 1949 Friedrich had obtained a first degree from Wagner College in New York and had done postgraduate work at the Mexican Escuela Nacional de Antropología e Historia. In Vienna he worked, like his

---

[5] Traverso, Enzo: Von der Frankfurter Schule zu Ernest Mandel. Fragestellungen und Sackgassen des Marxismus hinsichtlich Auschwitz, in: Traverso, Enzo: *Nach Auschwitz. Die Linke und die Aufarbeitung des NS-Völkermordes*, ISP Verlag, Köln 2000, 79-104, here 82.

[6] For Enrique Semo see David Mayer's article in this volume, fn. 13: *Der Weltenläufer: Friedrich Katz und die historiographischen Debatten seiner Zeit* [*Well-Versed in Worlds: Friedrich Katz and the historiographical debates of his time*].

[7] Rodolfo Stavenhagen (b. 1932) is a Mexican sociologist at El Colegio de México. He was Deputy Director General of UNESCO and, until 2008, the United Nations' first "Special Rapporteur on the situation of human rights and fundamental freedoms of indigenous people".

father, as a journalist for the *Volksstimme*,[8] a Communist daily, but his overriding priority was to pursue his studies of Mesoamerican history and in 1954 he graduated with a thesis on the economy of the Pre-Columbian Aztecs.

At this point we want to focus on the moment when Friedrich Katz published his first work on the Mexican Revolution, which he did in East Berlin. Katz moved to the German Democratic Republic in 1956, when de-Stalinization had just become the order of the day in the Soviet Union but had not yet filtered through to all parts of Central and Eastern Europe. The SED (Socialist Unity Party of Germany) leadership remained especially averse to reform. Only four years earlier a member of the Central Committee of the SED, Alexander Abusch, who had himself been in exile in Mexico, had denounced Leo Katz and others as representatives of a "Jewish-chauvinistic tendency".[9] In the Stalinist context, open references to the Holocaust and Germany's historic responsibility, important set pieces of political propaganda though they were, tended to acquire an anti-Zionist edge. Abusch himself was forced to resign from his various functions for a time in 1950 because of the Merker case. Khrushchev's recent denunciation of Stalin at the 20th Party Congress of the CPSU in 1956 was yet to produce any changes in the political climate in the GDR. In spite of all this, Katz moved to Berlin where he worked at the Humboldt University until the late 1960s. In 1962 he completed his habilitation thesis, which he devoted to the Mexican Revolution, and published it in 1964 as *Deutschland, Diaz und die mexikanische Revolution* (*Germany, Diaz and the Mexican Revolution*).[10] On its evidence and on the evidence of other publications from these years[11] it transpires that Katz was among the very first to draw attention to another German telegram that was to trigger consequences on a global scale: German Foreign Minister Arthur Zimmermann's cable of January 19, 1917, in which he tried to make an alliance with Germany palatable to the Mexican government in the event of the USA entering the war, the prize with which he tempted the Mexicans being Texas, New Mexico and Arizona. The cable had an incomparably

---

[8] Leo Katz wrote for the *Volksstimme* until his death in 1954 – 14 months before the withdrawal of the Red Army from Austria and before the Stalinplatz was given back its old name of Schwarzenbergplatz.

[9] Herf, Jeffrey: *Divided Memory: The Nazi Past in Two Germanys*, Harvard University Press, Cambridge 1997, 135.

[10] Katz, Friedrich: *Deutschland, Diaz und die mexikanische Revolution: Die deutsche Politik in Mexiko 1870–1920* (=Schriftenreihe des Instituts für Allgemeine Geschichte an der Humboldt-Universität Berlin 9), Deutscher Verlag d. Wissenschaften, Berlin 1964.

[11] Katz, Friedrich: Alemania y Francisco Villa, in: *Historia Mexicana* 12 (1962), 88-102.

greater effect on US policy than Riegner's above-mentioned message: it is considered the last straw in Woodrow Wilson's decision-making process leading to the United States declaring war on Germany.

It becomes apparent here how Katz' indefatigable interest in international history and in both diachronous and synchronous global comparisons is ultimately angled towards the Mexican Revolution. During the revolutionary period, Germany appeared as a leading actor on the international stage, which had previously been dominated by Mexico's northern neighbour, the USA, and by Great Britain and France. In his attempts to identify historical patterns underlying the catastrophes of the recent past, Katz did not confine himself to variations on the question of the responsibility for the war, a discussion that had been gaining ground again from 1945 onwards; he went further. In 1966 he published a book on German fascism in Latin America, which also appeared in Mexico in 1968.[12] In a way he mirrors the method of his father, who, during the war, had used the stories of well-known antifascists to denounce the crimes of an infernal regime. In his capacity as historian, the son contributed to the scholarly efforts of his time to understand the "internationalism" of the Nazis by drawing on sources that had by then become part of history.

It looks like a dialectical coincidence that almost exactly 30 years later another erstwhile Mexican exile, who had by then taken up residence in another country, turned the tables once again. In his novel *Nazi Literature in the Americas* the Chilean writer Roberto Bolaño, for whom his sojourn in Mexico proved a formative experience, created a fictional universe of Nazi literature to unmask contemporary totalitarian tendencies in Latin America.[13] The Bolaño of 1996, as one of his reviewers noted, "draws on the referentiality of events to invent history".[14] The Friedrich Katz of 1966 makes events refer to the significance that is due to them in terms of global history. Both men found refuge at crucial moments in their youth in Mexico to escape from dictatorship and certain death.[15] Both men kept visiting in later life the socio-political constellations that formed the basis of the transnational significance of this particular

[12] Katz, Friedrich/Sanke, Heinz (eds.): *Der Deutsche Faschismus in Lateinamerika 1933–1943*, Humboldt-Universität zu Berlin, Berlin 1966. Katz, Friedrich (ed.): *Hitler sobre América Latina: el fascismo alemán en Latinoamérica 1933–1943. 4 investigaciones históricas*, Fondo de Cultura Popular, México, D.F. 1968.

[13] Bolaño, Roberto: *Nazi Literature in the Americas*, New Directions Books; New York 2008. Bolaño, Roberto: *La literatura nazi en las Américas*, Seix Barral, Barcelona 1996.

[14] Peiró, José Vincente: ¿Quién puede comprender mi terror mejor que usted?, in: *Turia* 75/9 (2005), 211-214, here 212 [my translation].

[15] This is not meant to imply a structural comparison of any kind between National Socialism and the ideology of the Pinochet regime.

version of Mexico. Both men empathized enthusiastically with diverse protagonists of the revolution and they shared, if from highly different perspectives, a fascination with the US-Mexican border region.

Why are we devoting so much space to this particular stage of the historian Friedrich Katz' life and work? What justifies linking him to Bolaño? There are several answers to these questions. For one thing, it is at this stage that the transnational analysis of historical interrelations, which was to become Katz' hallmark, puts in its first appearance – without, incidentally, diminishing his attention to micro-historical accuracy in his study of the sources. And bearing in mind Bolaño's fictional books and authors, we may also recall a revealing episode in which Leo Katz, having got hold of a list of subscribers to the German *Nationalzeitung* in Mexico, produced an entire issue of the paper and had it printed and delivered to its Nazi friendly readers, who were predictably in for a shock. These details, significant though they are, should not obscure a far more important similarity between these two intellectuals, who, to my knowledge, never met in person.

In the last interview Bolaño gave shortly before his death in 2003 he was asked, "Are you Chilean, Spanish or Mexican?" He replied, "I am Latin American."[16] In April 2000 Roberto Bolaño visited Vienna, where the controversial coalition of the Christian Democrat Wolfgang Schüssel and the rightwing extremist FPÖ had been in power for two months, to take part in the conference "Europa – Lateinamerika: Literatur, Migration und Identität". He gave a reading from his novel *La literatura nazi* at the Instituto Cervantes and was invited to dinner at the Mexican embassy, "where the ambassador [...] kindly treated me as if I were Mexican".[17] And he delivered his well-known *Vienna Address*, entitled *Literature and Exile* – he consistently used the term "expulsion" in connection with exile lest this type of "exile" was confused with voluntary emigration – in which he remarked that "my homeland consists of my son and my books" because "the working man neither can nor should [feel nostalgia]: his hands are his homeland."[18]

---

[16] Bolaño, Roberto: The Last Interview (with Mónica Maristain), in: Bolaño, Roberto: *The Last Interview and Other Conversations*, Melville House, New York 2009, 93-123, here 99.

[17] Bolaño, Roberto: Vienna and the Shadow of a Woman, in: Bolaño, Roberto: *Between parentheses. Essays, Articles and Speeches 1998–2003* (edited by Ignacio Echevarría), New Directions Books, New York 2011, 270-274, here 273.

[18] Bolaño, Roberto: Literature and Exile, in: Bolaño, Roberto: *Between parentheses. Essays, Articles and Speeches 1998–2003* (edited by Ignacio Echevarría), New Directions Books, New York 2011, 38-45, here 42.

What is fascinating here is that Friedrich Katz has also been made the subject of an essay that employs the device of fictional parallel lives to approach the historicity of his life. The author, the historian Mauricio Tenorio, recounts an incident in an academic setting, in which

> "a rather stuck-up historian urged [Katz] to answer her question. 'And what about you, Friedrich? Would you say you're a Mexican, a German or a US-American?' Professor Katz simply pointed out that he had never been a German national, he was an Austrian, if anything, and was full of admiration for Mexico, the country he and his family owed their lives to, but: 'if I have to give an answer to this question I would say that I'm a survivor, I'm one of those who've been able to extricate themselves'."[19]

Katz a survivor? The avowal may come as a surprise. To be sure, Enrique Semo reminded his audience at the launch of the *Festschrift* for Friedrich Katz at Columbia University in November 2010 that Katz and he himself belonged to the "same generation of survivors". On the same occasion Adolfo Gilly quoted the above-mentioned episode as recounted by Tenorio, adding that Katz' words had "come from the heart". He also added that "the meaning [Katz] attached to his own biography" remained an open question.[20] However that may be, the category of survivor is arguably indispensable for an understanding of the great historian and teacher, whose importance for the historiography of several epochs and several regions of Latin America is impossible to overstate. Despite his exile and his life on the move, whose prime motivation had been the need to escape from fascism, and despite his being dealt a double share of Nazi terror – his family being Jewish and Communist – he is not usually seen as a survivor. Maybe this is to do with the fact that the term often appears in tandem with that of the victim, a person who is deprived of all initiative almost by definition. Friedrich Katz has demonstrated that this need not be the case.

Art Spiegelman called the famous comic in which he recounts the story of his father's survival in and after the time of the Holocaust, *Maus. A Survivor's Tale*. The title has been variously interpreted by literary critics but there seems to be general consensus that it does refer to mice and to the fact that this species is under threat from an infinitely more powerful and lethal species. In Spiegel-

[19] Tenorio Trillo, Mauricio: Vidas Imaginarias, in: Garciadiego, Javier/Kourí, Emilio (eds.): *Revolución y exilio en la historia de México. Del amor de un historiador a su patria adoptiva: Homenaje a Friedrich Katz*, ERA/University of Chicago/El Colegio de México, México, D.F./Chicago 2010, 89-104, here 90 [my translation].

[20] Quoted from the video recording of the event in: http://www.youtube.com/watch?v=ktrHM03lp88 (retrieved on May 22, 2012).

man's comic, cats in the guise of the German Nazis are working towards the extinction of the "Jewish mice". Spiegelman was not the first to conceive the empowering of mice and equip them with an indomitable sense of initiative, which banks, against all odds, on the possibility of changing the world for the better: Leo Katz had already claimed "Maus" as a journalistic pseudonym for himself in Berlin during the Weimar Republic. The analogy is valid even though the name Katz, being derived from Kohn or Cohen, is etymologically unrelated to cat (German *Katze*). The activist mouse survives the Armageddon orchestrated by the cats and retains for the future not only his interest in the social structures of the world but a "deep-seated historical optimism".[21] Friedrich Katz shared both these traits with his father and, what is more, he used them as factors that shaped his work as a historian.

In the above-mentioned function at Columbia, Claudio Lomnitz put Katz' perspective on Mexican history under that same aspect:

> "Mexico's twentieth century was shaped by exile. Friedrich is probably the person who has seen this most clearly first and foremost. First, the exile of Mexicans [...] and then Mexico as a place that received exiles, exiles who contributed to shaping Mexico in the imagination. Friedrich was one of these exiles, and he had the peculiarity of writing a history of Mexico that de-centered the national narrative as only an exile can do. Showing consistently similarities between Mexico and other places in the world, looking for international connections and demonstrating their significance even for the keystone event of Mexico's modern history, which is its social revolution at the beginning of the twentieth century."

Lomnitz went on to say that what sets Friedrich Katz' oeuvre apart from other diplomatic histories is the fact that, as an author, he has no privileged perspective; he eschews alike a Mexican, a German and a US point of view. The history of international relations and the regional history of the border country are "synthesized in Friedrich's work, bringing together diplomatic, social and political history in a way that only an exile could hope to accomplish. There is no privileged identification."[22] Katz wrote about Mexico from a distance, even if it was always bridged by empathy, and that distance was not merely due to the fact that his writing desk happened to be in Austria, Germany or the United States at that

---

[21] Kloyber, Christian: México/Datos biográficos, in: Douer, Alisa/Seeber, Ursula (eds.): *Qué lejos está Viena. Latinoamérica como lugar de exilio de escritores y artistas austríacos*, Forschungs- und Dokumentationsstelle für Neuere Österreichische Literatur, Wien 1995, 112 [my translation].

[22] Quoted from the video recording of the event in: http://www.youtube.com/watch?v=ktrHM03lp88 (retrieved on May 22, 2012).

particular time. Katz' empathetic distance was the result of his authentic cosmopolitanism based on historical criticism. In that sense Lomnitz compared Friedrich Katz' perspective on global history with that of other expelled Austrians of his calibre like Eric Wolf and Eric Hobsbawm.

How can we best define the extent to which Katz' personal biography informed his type of historical analysis? Let me quote Claudio Lomnitz once more, who wrote about the Katz family in general and about Friedrich in particular:

> "They were protected by the Mexican consul in Marseille – Gilberto Bosques – and brought to Mexico as political exiles. In other words, Katz' defense of the Mexican Revolution was also personal, and this made him beloved as a Mexican. [...] But Katz also belonged to an academic generation [...] in which he represented minority concerns – sometimes as a Jew, sometimes as a Communist, sometimes as a European who thought that Mexico and its Revolution had something to teach the world."[23]

It was Friedrich Katz together with Christian Kloyber who made sure in June 2003 that the City of Vienna named a footpath near the UN Headquarters after Gilberto Bosques: a positive intervention into the sometimes problematic politics of history concerning the city's public space. And it was an opportunity for Katz to demonstrate his gratitude to the Mexican diplomat who had saved tens of thousands, including the Katzes, from certain death.

Towards the end of his great book on Pancho Villa and his time Friedrich Katz tells an anecdote featuring Villa, who, thanks to a 1935 Hollywood film, became an important role model for young Austrian Socialists in their struggle against the austrofascist dictatorship. He concludes that story by saying that in the mid-19th century "an Austrian, Maximilian of Habsburg, had gone to Mexico to set up an authoritarian empire. Now, in one of history's ironies, the image of a Mexican revolutionary, in the shape of Pancho Villa, had come to Austria and became an instrument of democratic struggle in that country."[24] In another historical turnabout Friedrich Katz made sure that Consul Gilberto Bosques received at least belated commemorative honours in the city of Katz' birth, where he himself had experienced the all too common anti-Semitism against survivors upon his return in 1949. (And where, in yet another volte-face, albeit under infi-

---

[23] Lomnitz, Claudio: On the Improbable Popularity of Friedrich Katz, in: *Estudios Mexicanos* 27/1 (2011), 233-239, here 237 and 239.

[24] Katz, Friedrich: *The Life and Times of Pancho Villa*, Stanford University Press, Stanford 1998, 818.

nitely less existential circumstances, another hospitable diplomat made Roberto Bolaño a Mexican for one night.) A few weeks after Friedrich Katz' interment in the new Jewish graveyard in Vienna in the autumn of 2010, Adolfo Gilly said of his late friend: "The one who survived is now back in Vienna."[25] Here, maybe more than anywhere else, we are called upon to try and make sense of the many twists of his life and survival.

[25] Quoted from the video recording of the event in: http://www.youtube.com/watch?v=ktrHM03lp88 (retrieved on May 22, 2012).

Autorin und Autoren

Javier Garciadiego (*jagarcia@colmex.mx*)

Der Historiker und führende Experte für die Geschichte der Mexikanischen Revolution ist Präsident von El Colegio de México und Mitglied der Historischen Akademie Mexikos. Der Betreuer seiner zweiten Dissertation an der University of Chicago war Friedrich Katz.

Historian and leading expert on the history of the Mexican Revolution, president of El Colegio de México and a member of the Mexican Academy of History. His advisor for his second dissertation at the University of Chicago was Friedrich Katz.

Martina Kaller (*kallerm9@univie.ac.at*)

Philosophin und Historikerin, Präsidentin des 54. International Congress of Americanists (54. ICA) an der Universität Wien vom 15. bis zum 20. Juli 2012. Im Sommersemester 2012 Gastprofessorin am Pablo Neruda-Chair an der Université Sorbonne Nouvelle – Paris 3.

Philosopher and historian, president of the 54th International Congress of Americanists (54th ICA) at the University of Vienna, 15–20 July 2012. During the summer term of 2012 visiting professor at the Pablo Neruda Chair at the Université Sorbonne Nouvelle – Paris 3.

Christian Kloyber (*christian.kloyber@bifeb.at*)

Der Germanist und Geograph leitet das Geschäftsfeld Bildungsentwicklung am Bundesinstitut für Erwachsenenbildung in Strobl am Wolfgangsee, Salzburg. Seit 1975 beschäftigt er sich mit der Dokumentation und Erforschung des deutschsprachigen Exils in Mexiko.

Germanist and geographer. Director of Education Development at the Bundesinstitut für Erwachsenenbildung (Federal Institute for Adult Education) in Strobl/Wolfgangsee, Salzburg. Since 1975, he has been working on the documentation and analysis of the German speakers' exile in Mexico.

David Mayer (*david.mayer@univie.ac.at*)

Historiker an der Universität Wien, Arbeitsschwerpunkte: Historiographiegeschichte, Geschichte des Marxismus sowie Geschichte sozialer Bewegungen. Eingehende Forschungen zu marxistisch inspirierten Geschichtsdebatten in Lateinamerika in den ‚langen 1960er Jahren'. Zur Zeit Generalsekretär des 54. International Congress of Americanists.

Historian at the University of Vienna. Main areas of interest are the history of historiography, the history of Marxism, and the history of social movements. Has carried out extensive research on the Marxist historical debates conducted in Latin America in the 'long 1960s'. Currently Secretary General of the 54th International Congress of Americanists.

Berthold Molden (*berthold.molden@univie.ac.at*)

Historiker an der Universität Wien, arbeitet zur Ideen- und Ideologiegeschichte des globalen Antikolonialismus im 20. Jahrhundert und zu geschichtspolitischen Kontroversen des Kalten Krieges in Europa und den Amerikas. 2012–2013 Gastprofessor (Marshall Plan-Chair) an der University of New Orleans.

Historian at the University of Vienna, who works on the intellectual and ideological history of global anticolonialism in the twentieth century and on the politics of history in Europe and the Americas during and after the Cold War. 2012–2013 visiting professor (Marshall Plan Chair) at the University of New Orleans.

Wiener Vorlesungen:
Forschungen

Herausgegeben für die Kulturabteilung der Stadt Wien
von Hubert Christian Ehalt

Band 1 Julian Uher: Systembedingte Arbeitslosigkeit – alternative Beschäftigungspolitik. 2000.

Band 2 Michael Lang: Die Rechtsprechung des EuGH zu den direkten Steuern. Welcher Spielraum bleibt den Mitgliedstaaten? 2007.

Band 3 Wolfgang Neugebauer / Kurt Scholz / Peter Schwarz (Hrsg.): Julius Wagner-Jauregg im Spannungsfeld politischer Ideen und Interessen – eine Bestandsaufnahme. Beiträge des Workshops vom 6. / 7. November 2006 im Wiener Rathaus. 2008.

Band 4 Peter Landesmann: Der Antijudaismus auf dem Weg vom Judentum zum Christentum. 2012.

Band 5 Peter Landesmann: Anti-Judaism on the Way from Judaism to Christianity. 2012.

Band 6 Martina Kaller / David Mayer / Berthold Molden (Hrsg.): Friedrich Katz. Essays zu Leben und Wirken eines transnationalen Historikers. Essays on the Life and Work of a Transnational Historian. 2012.

www.peterlang.de